P9-DBO-584

Pradakshina

TRAVELS IN INDIA

Madhoor Kapur

*to monsoon bob
ravi & chetan
with warmth
and love
madhoor '03*

BLUEJAY BOOKS

An imprint of Srishti Publishers & Distributors
New Delhi & Calcutta

BLUEJAY BOOKS
An imprint of Srishti Publishers & Distributors
64-A, Adhchini
Sri Aurobindo Marg
New Delhi 110 017
srishtipublishers@forindia.com

Copyright © Madhoor Kapur 2002

ISBN 81-87075-76-7
Rs. 195.00

Cover Paintings by the author
Design: arrt@vsnl.com

Printed and bound in India by
Saurabh Print-O-Pack, Noida

All rights reserved. No part of this publication may
be reproduced, stored in a retrieval system, or transmitted,
in any form or by any means, electronic, mechanical,
photocopying, recording or otherwise,
without the prior written permission of the Publishers.

Dedication to Gapu

Contents

Preface

The geographical area of India is pictured poetically as a temple compound. The Himalayas to the north constitute the torana; the pradakshina, or sacred perambulation is in the clockwise direction starting in the east and moving along the adisthaan downwards to the tip of the country, and then up on the western side. The garbhagriha is placed in Khajuraho, with its entrance from Varanasi that is the mahamandapa, while the area of Rajasthan makes the mandapa. The book moves roughly along these lines, many places being visited and written about through personal impressions.

The Blue Desert

The Blue Desert

The bazaar burgeons with activity, but guards a railway station within itself like an unrevealed core. Beyond it, a metalloid path leads to the sea, a blue flash on bland dunes. The broad beach slopes downwards and one cannot hear the waves. It is a silent sea; its sound has been swept in afternoon murmurs and in the breeze.

A beggar musician stands at the restaurant hut and plucks on his instrument, his face angular, withered and dark. A serving boy places a coin before him; just another chore performed in his busy routine of running to and fro, washing plates, depositing banana leaves laden with rice and dal on tables, providing dripping drinks and collecting change from customers. The beggar accepts the coin matter-of-factly, concealing it in a pouch with his knobby fingers. Perhaps he comes to a place only once. Would he never walk once again into this street, into this town? Or does he show up every day, and was it that which makes the transaction so mundane? He goes out into the dust and open sunlight, leaving the restaurant to its habitual and humdrum activity.

The narrow and crooked streets lead past dilapidated buildings to a large square. It is astir with people, rickshaws, scooters and hawkers, cars and carts. The ancient temple protrudes from the façade of small shops like a mountain of rock. An enormous triangle of saffron cloth flaps at its peak in the sea breeze. The sea cannot be seen. Here is a different world, ruled by the passion of human beings for their god. In that fervour superstition mixes with commerce; it is a bazaar of the soul with its own unmistakable festivity and thrift, adoration and hope. It is all too human, and has existed for generations. It is a meeting place that has not changed in character, but which has grown gradually in both stature and sanctity.

Pundits weave in and out of the crowd of beggars and pilgrims at the door, and can be spotted bare-chested and lungi-clad, sacred threads over their torsos and sandalwood marks on their foreheads. They have assumed this attire for hundreds of years, and it has ensured not only respectability and honour, but a livelihood for their class as well. Beggars and lepers wait for alms from pilgrims, and for solace from their god. The signs they wear on their impoverished bodies are the broken limbs that give them their livelihood. Worldly visitors emerge from the sanctums with compassion and generosity etched across their faces. They have completed a cycle of karma in this life with the darshan of the deity within. There is free food for all that come, at all times. The very gaze of god has touched donations of grain and money from rich and poor alike. On festival days, hundreds of thousands are fed. Nevertheless, one can come to the temple completely empty-handed. One can even sit in askance like the beggars: that too would fall within the aura of compassion of the deity who looks upon all equally without caste distinction. This tradition has endured uniquely in this temple for centuries. On the faces of the suffering and the poor at the gates is also written the belief that to be born human, no matter how beset with problems, is in itself the highest blessing, the highest good. Many come with much hardship from all corners of the land and from far away. They wait in silence at the doors for a momentary tryst with their god. And they come away, invariably receiving the god's own benediction, because they approach him so very simply. More than merely becoming blessed, they imbue their lives with deep meaning through this simple act. The deity is the supreme avatar of the age of Kalyug, carved by Vishvakarma himself. The craftsman god has made the deity without hands or feet, and left him incomplete, to indicate that he can be of no help to humanity in this most difficult of eras. Despite this, the god Jaggannath, as he is known, succeeds in comforting each man in the sea of humanity that comes to him in wave after wave, year after year.

It has always been hard to distinguish the good from the bad in the world, yet there seems to be no hypocrisy at the temple doors: what appears really is. It is only a question of being able to see. One has to be innocent to see the pilgrims as they really are; one needs openness to feel the cleanness of the sea breeze as one walks away to the shore. It takes both time and courage to come away from dust and heat to water. Perhaps it even dilutes one's conviction of what is right and wrong. If one's mind wavers, it is because it has been nurtured too long in an everyday world, for the mind behind the temple doors is indeed timeless. One is free to walk away, but somewhere along one's path, one will come across the man who played music in the teashop. Perhaps he had become a musician for only a day. Then one views his instrument slung across the shoulder like another sacred thread. He is striding into the shadows of the street, avoiding both the harsh sun and the overwhelming glare of the temple. One day, his old instrument might reveal a secret awakening to an inner dawn and a victory over ignorance. Is it imperative, one wonders, to have an instrument to keep a wholly accepted path at bay? Could a frail string and an empty gourd keep their integrity? Could the way of the pundit be reserved only for the others? In the labour of that music, there may be the power of the universe, or there may be nothing. What does it matter, if the player knows nothing about the game? Of what use is that knowledge to the intruder who has merely fallen in, aware? The part of oneself that one has given in sacrifice, whether one is pilgrim, pundit or beggar, results in a balance at the sanctum, and within that alone, each can survive. Yet to find joyousness within what lives is again a gift from the limbless god within.

There is always intense activity at the entrance, and within the precinct it continues, spreading everywhere within those walls. There are rows of stalls where one can buy food to offer the gods. There are lamp makers working with dry leaves to make cups and set them up with terracotta thimbles and cotton wool wicks, after filling them with marigold petals. Garland sellers squat in the temple bazaar; shops sell trinkets and souvenirs that replicate the building in clay and plastic miniatures. Other shops sell marble slabs, and will engrave the name of the buyer upon them to be donated to the courtyard's construction. There are even provision stores, and teashops with shelves full of sweets. There are cloth shops with the name of god printed on fabric. Baskets laden with puffed rice, condiments, savouries and sweets go in to become blessed, and the priests bring them out and return them to pilgrims, who guard them carefully to distribute to faraway relatives once they return home.

Many pundits within the temple approach visitors and question them on their caste, lineage and place of domicile. They keep records of families, and have done so for generations, each pundit having been assigned a particular clan. Beyond the wall of the courtyard, there are Banyan trees and stone slabs, many of which have the names of families inscribed upon them. The temple houses exquisite art, stone carvings that have remained unharmed through the passage of time. In places, the stone has crumbled, but there are also perfectly preserved sculptures of couples and demons, or musicians, high in the edifice of stone where the hands could not reach, and where the protection of the temple is invincible. The figures evoke the divine, soaring above a teeming humanity, the hundreds that lie or sit in the shade of pavilions bordering the inner sanctum. Among the masses are the ill and the crippled, and they have taken solace within the temple grounds. The inner sanctum remains closed behind brass doors and is heavily padlocked. It opens only at appointed times, but the worshippers sit patiently in clusters throughout the day, awaiting darshan. The sanctums are as dark and mysterious as caves, smoky with oil lamps and the fumes of camphor. Their very air is aged and seems to have the power to further constrict the space within. As the pilgrim comes again into the open courtyard, the sudden sunlight makes his eyes pucker, and the mystery of the dark space he has left behind only grows. The force of the temple rings out very far beyond the walls, and has done so ever since the first stones were laid so long ago. The unfinished god who had been wrought in anger by his maker in heaven has sent out his message of hope and blessing to millions of believers through time, ever since he took sanctuary in the heart of the temple. It is a message that rings true to this very day and endures because it touches each heart.

The sea glitters in one corner of the horizon, and is grey-blue ahead. The waves have immense force, the sky seems to tumble forward revealing white surf underneath which scatters in wide ribs at one's feet. Along the beach are silhouettes of passers-by. Women with large baskets on their heads and babies in their arms bob in the mirage, saris flapping in bold colours. There are men with enormous earthenware pots slung on strings from bamboo sticks, which are balancing on their shoulders. This gives their gait a curious lilt because the pots seem stationary as they move on the sand, weighed by the fish they contain. A man walks briskly, twining cotton wool on a metal spindle, with the spun string tucked under his arm. People walk silently. If they happen to be in small groups, their conversations become clipped by the recurrent rhythm of the tide. It erases the flow of sentences, which begins afresh in the lull. There is the rare cry of a seabird. A man walks into the waves and dips a wicker basket into the water. Sometimes there are children, gleeful and boisterous, in a separate harmony with the water. The movements of most people are parallel to the tide, which compels horizontality and turns whatever is upright into a dark stick. Very far away, a mass of dark dots glistens at the edge of water, and village huts lie beyond them. Fisherfolk are out in the afternoon. Boats are far out to sea; the wind has puffed out their sails like finely manicured fingernails that scrabble a delicate sky.

A young fisherman runs up to the waves, excitedly looking out to the choppy sea. He raises his hands above his forehead: half a mile out, he has spotted fish. He cries out to the others, who, until then, have sat placidly on the sands, drying the giant nets. His shout quickens their reflexes; they are instantly taut in frenzy. They deftly ground a boat shoreward, fixing oars upon it. They must speed before the harvest of fish escapes their nets. Their concern seems to charge the very air with electricity. Scarcely a minute has passed, and there are a score of hands on the vessel, a dozen muscular backs hoisting the boat, levering it upon oars that protrude from the sides. They tug and push slowly in perfect unison and ease the boat as it reaches the breakers. The boy who spotted the fish climbs aboard, and all the while shouts instructions to the rest. His shout rises above the furore of crossed decibels of all voices sounding simultaneously. Others waste no time in hauling the seemingly endless nets toward the boat. Each man holds one coil and walks in harmony with the others, so as not to knot up the carefully arranged nets. They are as one mind, these men. Some fetch large swirls of rope as the vessel passes the white hurdle of surf and rocks gently. The fishermen get on, unfasten the oars that have been tied down, and are soon maneuvering them over larger waves. Meanwhile, they position themselves in a familiar formation. The tide tosses the boat high and brings it down with a pendulum-like grace. It takes each man not only the experience taught from infancy, but also what is the legacy of generations, to wrest this perfection. The entire procedure has taken but a few moments. Soon, they are halfway to their spoil, a thick rope anchoring them to the shore. A tedious and meticulous tugging will haul in the giant nets, wriggling with a wealth of fish. The afternoon, which begins in a bang, will end in an evening's whimper. The fishermen will stand perpendicular to the sea and pull at the rope that ends in water. And as darkness will fall on their toil, it will wash in the teeming nets, the fruit of their labour.

There are few lampposts along the street, and the tiny cubicles that serve as shops are lit with oil lanterns; occasionally one comes to a shop lit by a weak electric light, displaying affluence despite its nakedness. There are provision stores with soaps and condiments stuffed into shallow wooden shelves in a vaguely systematic manner. Below them, boxes bulge with grain. The vegetable shops are just thatch and wall, and the aubergines and leeks, green leaves, onions and okra are spread on cloth or in baskets on the floor. A tiny box serves as the coconut seller's shop in the day, and is empty now except for the two men who gossip on its platform: the day has been a sellout, and the evening an abandonment. Stalls and teashops are the more prosperous ones, and have been there many years, judging by their concrete structures. Past a clearing that is hidden by trees, lamps glow and flicker a rich gold in the dark, inviting one to visit. There, fisherwomen sit behind tiny wooden boards displaying small fish. Further on, there are more stalls, their onions and tomatoes glistening like eggs and jewels. There is activity on the narrow road; pedestrians hobble to avoid the rickshaws. Under a Banyan tree, a cemented floor supports effigies and under its whitewashed trunk stands a black stone phallus. Dried garlands of marigold swing from branches and several men sprawl on the floor, exhausted limbs resting on their brows or tucked under their sleeping heads. The row of barbers who had clipped and soaped in the day has disappeared with its tin cases and wobbly mirrors, and the hawking ground is now a mere pile of stone slabs. A betel leaf seller crouches in a small cube, stirring lime paste to brush his leaves, into which he will wrap nuts, spices and the fragrant powders of his trade. He is as nimble-fingered as the woman who splits apart coconuts, and is only slightly more colourful with the jars of peanut candy and village sweets laid out behind him, his cubicle reeking of the dark cheroots he stocks. The egg shop hangs its solitary goods in wire baskets, and also lays them on racks upon a table. The night has lent the marketplace an enchantment, softening hawker cries and making conversations hum. Tinkling bicycles have the most persistent sound and are usually responsible for the scurrying of easy shoppers and loitering walkers.

The shrine by the road is small and gaudy. It is no more than a cement cupboard at the end of a platform, covered with a tin roof supported by pillars that are painted an awkward blue. An old Banyan tree slants through the roof and occupies the centre. About twenty men sit around the bright door of the shrine, chanting at the foot of the deity. Four pundits sit closer to him, each with cymbals in hand. Another man is on the harmonium, and behind him, someone beats on a drum. They have marked their foreheads and the bridges of the noses with sandalwood paste, and that has cracked over their wrinkles. Poverty has made their faces harsh and even brutal; the music they make has a sting, and in its fervour is adversity, lurking like a beast underneath the notes. Their old faces are sunken and deeply lined; here and there the white stubble of beards pushes vehemently, and startles one even in the weak electric light. There is a man who is fat, with puffy face and long oiled hair falling on his shoulders in grey curls. He presses on his instrument elatedly as the hymn rises into the air, along with the swirls of incense. Behind the men who chant sit a dozen others. Waifs strolling on the street are drawn in by the music as well. Heads move to the brisk rhythm and there is clapping. A few have leaned on pillars, their heads drooping as if in mourning. The children are awake even in the late night, their eyes bright and alive in the light of the god's oil lamp. There are trays of flowers near the shine of cymbals. A pundit reads from an old and tattered book, provoking conversation and more music. The entrance is guarded by two cement lions with yellow eyes that are larger than those of the waifs, and they have lashing vermilion tongues. Small paper fans and clusters of garlands seem to snuff out the black deity; the naked electric bulb throws the altar in stern shadows. Walls beyond the door are painted with kitsch angels, their hands folded in obeisance. The patio floor is heavy with the day's dust, and there the passer-by sits down in front of his god; perhaps he is merely resting his weary limbs. A smoking pipe is passed from person to person. As the pundits lift their eyes from the pages of the book, one sees that they are shot with red. The sandalwood tray is passed around; each man smears his forehead and leaves a coin. A rickshaw driver sits on the pavement for a short while, a woman more shriveled than her sari kneels at the door and lifts her two wet eyes and walks away. She carries in her gait all the tragedy of poverty, age and ignorance. Dogs amble past and no one throws a stone. A man wheezes deeply as he heaves himself off the floor. He stands rubbing his head and then disappears into the deserted street. Short hymns begin slowly, rise in a deafening din of voices, drum and cymbals, and end abruptly, as if aware of the late hour and the emptying road. A boy, tired from a long day's labour, stretches out beneath the pillar and is soon asleep, close to a wakeful god. A hundred yards away, train hoots into the station, exhaling steam that floats above the trees. The rickshaw drivers are alert to that sound and hurry off, the lame beggars hobble away, and the waifs are lured too, leaving only the fervent behind. And soon, their voices become muffled in the night, vanquished too by exhaustion.

The taxi drives through small streets of the town and reaches open spaces, going inland through green fields and forests of palm trees. The greenery is not everywhere; often, fields are bare and brown, and the sweeping wind carries dust. Canals give the landscape sheen. The taxi rattles onto mud to let buses overtake it. Crossing villages, one sees farmers bent over paddy crop, tending the oncoming harvest. As the taxi goes happily over the countryside, the driver talks incessantly. Suddenly, he stops in front of a group of boys and hurries out of the car. He grabs one of the bunch, harshly shouting at him. The boy immediately takes off his shirt and gives it to the driver. Wordlessly, the driver returns to the wheel, tosses the shirt on the back seat and resumes driving. A thief has been caught red-handed, flaunting a stolen shirt outside town. The incident is soon forgotten, and the taxi now halts before a level crossing. Buses and other vehicles soon pile on both sides of the track and passengers alight for a stroll or a drink of coconut water from roadside vendors. The wait lasts fifteen minutes, people become impatient, but there is no sign of a passing train. Then, in an anticlimax, a trolley with six men on its tiny platform scuttles past on the track, flapping two red triangular flags on the rollers. They have the air of important people, which only heightens the comic element in the scene. Lazily, the keepers of the crossing now lift the creaking poles upward, onlookers climb on to their vehicles, and, at long last, traffic moves on. Once again, the countryside of bare fields interspersed with greenery begins, spiked with the dark palm trees that rustle in the breeze.

Over the past thousand years, the sea has receded a few kilometres, but when the temple was built, it rested on the beach, the water lapping near its walls. Now it lies in palm groves and on sand dunes, and the stones have charred in the salty air. Perhaps time has hidden it effortlessly from the open sea, sky and stretching sands, preferring to nest it among trees like a treasure whose spire alone is visible from afar. The terrain has the effect of shrinking the temple in appearance: between treeline and dune, it seems toylike and innocent. Only as one walks towards it, does its magnificence and enormity become apparent. As one steps down into the courtyard of grass, a force descends from its high pinnacle. Adjacent structures have crumbled almost to their foundations, so that only the central temple now remains. There is also an adjoining entrance temple with rows of abandoned pillars that are still standing. Several areas in the vast courtyard are no more than raised patios. Under one of them, a Banyan tree sprouted hundreds of years ago, breaking through the granite floor and spreading a stubborn umbrella of shade. That too has been the effortless handiwork of time; yet perhaps a sculptor had foreseen all this and left a seed underneath the stone floors that he was to carve.

The twenty-four wheels of the temple have not stirred; the chariot-monument has remained immobile. It is nature that has moved away, using the illusion of time to beguile the eyes of men. Human eyes are millennia old, the hands of sculptors seem to say, and the works of the hand last longer than one's bones. Perfection does not ring true when the work is done, but plays with time and moulds it for its own messages. Even granite is frail against the gossamer spray of the sea that scatters in a single gust of breeze. The ephemeral foam has vanquished the firm mountain of rock; the shifting sands have won over the unshakable. The sole victory that remains with the makers is not their ritual or their wealth, but their love of beauty. Truth is still in the place of the mind, and nature has no path to that truth, but only one to its own powers. The mind through the hand has overcome the strong seas; the mind that released only the creation of the hands has overcome nature's vastness, which can let loose only a gentle spray. It is within the character of the mind to consecrate a shrine to the sun, to transfix upon the territory of earth, sea and sky, an unsurpassed jewel that reflects the splendour of the sun in an ornament upon the home of mind, the earth. At the very edge, where the mind bursts to fullest bloom, there is left nothing, save a pathless and incomprehensible nature. In its freedom, nature recedes within the prism of time. Nature is warped through time, as art is through the mind, and distortion fans out in a multicoloured spectacle even as imagination stirs reality. Time moves the sands and the limits of land.

The face of the rock is intricately carved with numerous figures of dancers, musicians and lovers. Panels are repeated geometrically over the rectangular structure that ascends in steps and gives way to a pyramid-like cupola. As the eyes move higher, there are deeply embossed figures and large niches with more figures. Areas below are filled with magnificent chimeras, their weight balanced by the angular ripple of carved rock that contains delicately patterned flowers and serpents, bowers and plainly checkered backdrops. Figures of female musicians stand in more strata of stone, becoming smaller as they move higher up. These are the figures that light in the first of dawn's rays. On ground level, enormous chariot wheels periodically break a lattice pattern of figures. The uniform texture of stone has become the colour of the earth, and is punctuated by several high niches. There, gods and beasts are seated, carved out of green marble. The granite has been eaten away, but marble has withstood time's corrosion. The complexion of green gods is still smooth, their limbs still shiny and features yet finely hewn; creases on the sides of nostrils become real, the eyelids and fingernails delicate, heads of animals splendid and ferocious, all finely etched with measured stabs of sensitive chisels. At the main entrance, there remain two fearful monsters, agape and crumbling; and portions of stallions lie strewn, decaying on the grass.

The interior of the temple had been filled in by a far-sighted official of an earlier century. Human imagination has soared very high in the making of the temple, and that has been coupled with precision and practicality. When the emperors had wanted horses for the chariot, they were given divine beasts, and the monsters the sculptors made provoked both awe and admiration. In that perfection there was no disdain of the natural world into which the temple had been set: it matched instead the grandeur of the elements. For the moment, the monument became an artifact of mankind, the kings and artists who shaped it becoming mere instruments to its message and being. Even the love for an omnipotent god became, for that instant, a reason for the splendour and joy of sheer creativity. The entrance has been closed for all time, and art is no longer subject to a human will. A reality of stone overwhelms in the deserted courtyard. Countless hands have fashioned with one end in view over many years of passion and toil, and this can never fail to move the visitor.

The bus fills, and people are still getting on when the driver blows the horn to move. There are still some empty seats, and in the rudeness that ensues from there being more passengers than seats, there is a young boy who retains his politeness. He is different even in appearance to the rest. He wears clean white clothes and a crisp cap, yet could not be any better off. As the bus starts dustily, he starts a conversation with his neighbour. He has visited his father in the village and is now returning to his mother. Each sentence seems tempered with goodness; almost each sentence begins with the name of god. God had thought it best that this be so; when he speaks of his poverty, he says that god had sent it, and when he displays fear at the meanness of people, he says that these people are not precious to god. An innocence and gentleness marks each phrase, and a joy that goes beyond mere cheerfulness. In the middle of hardship and youth, there is a surpassing thankfulness. He is proud and accepts no favour, yet there is no harshness in his rejection. He would have said that god would wish for his circumstances to remain unchanged. One would feel that god decreed so after much care, nevertheless. One wishes for his god to protect him from the greedy world. Could one learn to accept in spite of the pride in one's destiny, and was that the making of a man? When the bus stopped at his mother's village, he left and was soon lost in the crowd. There was a clean white cap in the blur of dark and sunny heads. He left behind a radiant smile that lingered for a while after the bus had moved on.

From the beach, it looks like a ghost town. The wide sands have no trees, and the beach's mottled texture is the result of countless footprints, ending where large houses stand. These are heavy brick structures, and the breeze stirs through their empty arches aimlessly. A few palm trees grow within compounds, and behind the line of houses, a green treeline stretches to the horizon. The buildings are placed at odd angles to the uniform sand, and look out on the water with large, vacant windows and open-mouthed doors that are monotonous with flaking plaster. The beach heightens something sad in the structures and hints of solitude. If the fisherfolk did not have that constant air of preoccupation, working on their nets, sitting in groups, or walking purposefully with basketloads of fish, they too would assume the aura of very lonely ghosts. Their villages begin where these once stately homes diminish, the drab brown-grey cluster of huts relieved by dapper flags swung on sloping poles and abandoned boats.

There are few people on the beach. Further, there is a clearing against the vacant town. Here are scores of tiny local hotels, stuck wall to wall behind the beachfront road. Tourists to the temple spend a night or two here. They take their holy dip immediately in front of their hotel, accompanied by fishermen who guide them through the breakers. This area of the beach is busy. Hawkers sell trinkets, belts, pouches and strings of shell and coral. The blue expanse beyond is flecked with sails slanting in the swift wind. Nevertheless, the cleanness of the sea is forgotten in the bazaars, where there seem to be too many people, cycles and rickshaws, and the streets too narrow to sustain the anarchy that ensues. Clusters of swifts hover over a small shrine, the fluttering web of sharp tails and black wings making exhilarating arabesques in the bright morning air. Dark boats on the sands appear like moths that come to life at the touch of water. The feet of pilgrims lap the overflowing waves along the ochre ribbon that is no wider than a no-man's land, and seems hewn from both future and past. The beach is like a present time that wavers and flickers alternately glossy and matte, mirror-like in daylight. Tiny sandpipers and gulls are oblivious to the frailty of the ribbon of sand; further on, dozens of crows seem to rule raucously over it. Fish is brought in from boats and the squabbling voices of women rise above the turmoil of the tide. Yet underneath this, there is a silence that forever rests, undisturbed and pristine.

The small streets of the town are empty in the oppressive noon heat. The road is windless and dusty; the bazaars do not have their usual crowds. A boy walks his way to the vegetable and fruit shops, filling his bags with cucumbers and carefully chosen oranges. Four coconuts have the look of disheveled heads, and a mass of dates stick to each other, hot and sugary in the sun. He finds a poky wine shop that is open, and buys a flask that weighs down his bags. He stops for a drink of coconut water, as the hours in the heat have parched his throat. An old man reaches out for the greenest coconut in the pile, and swings a hack knife upon it, chipping off the top to split the sphere of sweet water at its centre. There is undisguised brutality in his guillotine chop, and unsmilingly, he hands the boy the drink. He drinks swift and deep, leaving small change for the man, and moves on to the next shop to buy cheroots, cigarettes and matchboxes; his bags now bulge at the sides. He hires a rickshaw and hands the bags to the driver, and then goes deeper into the bylanes of the deserted town. He stops at a stall where a woman sits behind bundles of stitched leaves. These are the plates upon which his feast will be served, and he gets a dozen for a bright new coin. There is no papaya in the shops; the oranges will have to suffice. The bakery is far away on the other side of the town. He sweats in the hot sun, eyes smarting from the glare and the salt that has formed into beads upon his brow. The rickshaw takes him past railway tracks, past rice fields to the left. Along the other side are the tile roofs of the suburb. The driver takes many turns, and where the road turns into a mud path, the boy can smell the bakery in the hot wind. He soon halts in front of a door that has no sign upon it, but there is the aroma of freshly baked bread. The unlit rooms are dismal, and a few dark men go about busily, their eyes flashing in the glare of the open door. There are roomfuls of loaves on racks, soft and complacent in their incubators. The owner comes up to the boy and apologizes for the darkness. Are there rolls, buns and cakes? There are none today because of the electricity failure, but there is bread, still warm and breathing from the ovens.

Then, it is a journey back to the town, to the edge of the beach where the fishing village begins. The rickshaw stops in its tracks, unable to pull in the sand. The boy alights, cautioning the driver to keep guard over his shopping, and goes down to the sea to buy fish. The driver had been enjoying the excursion, and has gone from one shop to the next gleefully. This familiarity annoyed the boy, and more than once he had reprimanded the driver to keep to his place and watch over his purchases, instead of following him laughingly into every shop. The driver stood hurt and morose at those words, but his expression would change in a childlike manner each time more bags would be piled into the rickshaw. The boy now found his way into the village, returning in half an hour with six fish gleaming on a string. The light of the sky was in his eyes, his hair was windblown, his shirt and trousers wrinkled in the sea breeze. He leaves the fish at a bamboo hut with instructions for them to be cooked by the evening. He then hastens to the market at the dead end of the road, climbing into the rickshaw after nudging the sleeping driver awake. On the dusty path, he asks for the woodchopper's hut. It is not far down the track, and, motioning to the driver, he steps down and walks further. He stops at a few shops, and disappears down an alley. A hut is stacked with neatly cut wood along the walls and the mud floor is littered with splinters and shavings. In the late afternoon, the wood smells fresh and dry. The boy rummages through the piles, taking fine sticks and heavier logs on a cloth to carry back. The old man puts the wood on primitive scales, balancing it against iron weights. The boy would need help hauling it to the rickshaw, so the man calls out to his son to help carry the load.

The overflowing rickshaw hobbles bumpily through the lanes. The driver is aglow with the air of festivity that the boy has unwittingly woven around himself. He is soon at the gates of his house, and wearily goes in, sending bearers to carry the things in and to pay off the rickshaw man. The sun spills gold on the sands not far away. He would rest, bathe, and put on fresh clothes for his feast.

The wood and food is carried to the beach, and the cloth and mats are laid. Darkness falls upon the sea swiftly. While there has still been some light, a hole has been dug in the sand, and the wood piled on it to start a fire. The wind is fierce and low. The boy tries to light the fire without success, and a man appears out of the surrounding dark and walks towards the threesome from the direction of the waves, offering to help. Paper at the bottom of the pit catches fire, and the man dexterously piles twigs on the flames, wincing in the salt-laden breeze. The four gather close to protect the fragile wisps of flame. Once the fire has caught, they set mats around it, careful not to let the sand settle on dishes. The man is from the police, and eyes the food and drink suspiciously. However, he only smiles when he is told that today is a day of feasting. The waves spread out like fans nearby, flat and ringed in foam that glistens in the half-moonlight.

The three sit down to their dinner. A dog wanders near, drawn by the warmth of flickering flames on the wide expanse of sand. He remains loyal for the whole evening, happy for the crumb tossed his way, or the fish bones that miss the fire but land on the sand near his paws. Three fishermen come from the village, their faces distraught with concern. The boy reassures them that the fire is far from their boats and nylon nets, and that it has been lit by the policeman himself. They seem pacified, but to dispel their fears, the boy hands them three oranges. There are people walking by in the dark, returning home from a long day's toil. The policeman has become a dark silhouette not too far away, and there seems to be another figure near

23

him. A little later, a girl crosses past, a mysterious figure in a fluttering dress and wild hair. An old fisherman comes by accompanied by a young boy, and they squat squarely by the fireside. The boy gives the old man wine that he drinks down, after giving it an inquisitive sniff. Judging from the instant wrinkles on his grimace, he far prefers his country liquor to this strange potion. With a heave and a shrug, and motioning to the boy beside him, he lifts himself up. He raises his arms above his head in greeting, and it turns into a gesture of merely adjusting the scarf on his head, as they move away. There is a singing voice that veers close enough, but then turns away and goes towards the village. The foam is nearly fluorescent and warm in the fierce wind of night. The three wade into the dark water, heads light with wine, bodies resilient in the midnight air. The unpredictable currents, the roar of waves that sharpens in the dead of night brings a fear that leaves the sea unused at night. The boy wonders how many people roam the beach at night. How does the fire appear to them, and what do they make of their laughter? He lies down on the hard sand, thinking that he has stepped on crabs. The fire crackles buoyantly in the distance, and the three run up to its flames. The cakes are sweet and fine mixing with the mineral saltiness of their wet fingers and mouths.

A path has been cleared in the fisher's village, and shops have sprung up on its sides over the years, but it always has the look of something makeshift that can be destroyed in an afternoon. Everything their simple lives require can be bought here; yet curiously, there is nowhere to buy fishing nets, ropes or hooks. There are bamboo stalls with shaky roofs and common walls, and in them sit vegetable sellers and betel nut vendors. There are provision shops and tailor establishments with cloths strung merrily and their owners sitting behind these flags, sewing on rattling machines. In the late afternoon the fisherwomen come in from the beach that is not far away, with basketfuls of fish and shrimp, and they lay them out on planks of wood by the road. A shop sells firewood, and a temple is also encased in a bamboo stall. There are teashops, and a barber has raised his cabin on wooden pegs and has the brightest shop because of the mirrors on its walls. There is always somebody who needs his hair clipped or his head massaged, but the other shops, in contrast, are always empty; there are only the owners gossiping with their coteries inside. There are scores of children, naked for the most part; occasionally one sees bright little triangles of loincloths on their dark bodies. The mothers sit with their children beside them, either combing their hair, or wiping their faces. Almost propped against the wall along with their handiwork is a family of basket weavers. The men split the bamboo poles and lay them before the womenfolk who mesh the baskets and the trays in which villagers sift grain. There is an ice factory in the middle of the village market, its compound filled with people washing fish under the taps in the corridors. The smell of fish is strong, and the workers are immune to it as they scrub and pack the fish into gunny sacks; occasionally, they sit down to the pungent cheroot smoke, sometimes passing it around and sometimes stubbing it short to save for the next session. At the end of small mud lanes, one can see the sea, a glistening blue blur; then once again, the goings-on of the market attract attention. A few of the shopkeepers prompt one into buying something and the young boys sitting on the benches grin and giggle, the women turn their heads away and cover them in modesty, somehow retaining a coquettishness. By and large, there is an unconcern between shoppers and owners, a lazy and pleasant rapport. Nothing unusual ever happens in the afternoon, and perhaps only the evenings bring on the habitual drunkards with their own brand of performance. The village is at the end of the town and yet strangely a world apart, unmixed with the plastic garishness of the more prosperous markets elsewhere.

It is a small shrine by the edge of water, and its pyramid dome is topped with a typical red flag. One approaches it from the narrow road, climbing the sand dune until one reaches the gently sloping steps that are bordered with a wall. A fat old man is the pundit of the shrine, a contented man with an air of quiet friendliness on a cherubic face and a beard that is shaved about once a week. There are also a couple of young Brahmins, who tend the shrine and the one adjacent, which lies on beach below. They are both dark and thin. When they are not with their god, they are in the marketplace, their Brahmin threads covered in nylon shirts and their white dhotis exchanged for trousers, bicycling through the crowds.

The shrine has weathered darkly by the sea, and bunches of periwinkles have caught at its foundation, like pink flames stuck in the sand. The shrine below has a natural spring, and there is always cool water in its stone bowl that never seems to bubble over. There are flowers set in the shallow water, and a pundit sits by the small monument under a flimsy canopy. In the afternoon and until the sun sets, there are hordes of pilgrims to both shrines. A hundred or more men and women and their children alight from buses and rickshaws and walk in the wind up the steps. They fold their hands and take a tour round the monument in the clockwise direction that is considered auspicious. They are just people from villages and theirs is a simple and blind faith, without the scars that come from prestige or honour. As the wind from the sea laps briskly at their clothes, they seem to be blessed with a benediction that comes only to those who have little. The colourful but impoverished saris of the women convulse wildly as they hold them over their heads, and the wind billows them out until they look like tossed flowers. The white dhotis of the men fill and their shirts starch crisply against their chests. Noserings and bangles shine on the women, and there is enthusiasm in their gait, the joy of a journey. The very shrine seems to become happy as they run against the wind to the shrine below, laughing and talking among themselves. The children all seem shaven clean, with only small tufts of hair in the back of their heads. They have large liquid eyes and radiant, easy smiles. The sun sets behind the trees, the clouds take the red and shoot it out in radial bands. There are little girls on the sides of their mothers, clutching boughs of flowers as they jostle downward to the shrine of the spring. One girl trips in the sand and her mother calls out to her, turning to help her on her feet once more; together, they run to the others who have already reached the lower shrine. There are old men, and younger men with gaunt heads, all with the air of people humbled in the presence of their god. They are direct in the acceptance of their god, and it is a beautiful thing. The simplicity of their circumstances shines clearly through that acceptance. As the crowd walks further to the waves, something within one is drawn and pulled along too. There is no fervour in them, only joy. A bouquet of breeze-blown flowers crushes towards the water, the light in the sky already changing, the water becoming grey and the sand monochrome, the foam fluorescent in the enigmatic dusk. Men and women wade into the waves up to their ankles and bend over to touch the water, the children following their elders with endearing mimicry. With wet fingers, they sprinkle water over their heads and fold their hands in prayer. For a moment, it is the sea that has become sacred with their touch. Their gesture has made it whole, a human soul has spoken to the vast being of the sea and a completeness of feeling has become known. A biological essence has worshipped and loved the earth, and known its beauty, and thanked. Some of the men fetch coins and give them to their sons to throw into the water. A group of naughty fisher boys gathers and hunts for the coins in the waves. And then, those darkening flowers return in the falling light to the sands by the shrine to sit by the spring. The pundit gathers them into a circle and recounts tales of the gods. Their eyes, in that twilight, drink in his words, their bodies taut in wonder. Their stillness before the storyteller is childlike; words become magical once again. Even the smiling children have stopped their pranks and merely dawdle on the laps of their mothers, quiet too, and spellbound under the voice that speaks with passion and authority. They are wonderful in their simplicity, and one wishes for them never to gain the complexity of understanding. Overhead, a cluster of swifts twitters in the breeze, wheeling over the pyramid dome. In the near darkness, the sea breeze and the voice on the sands gently lull the mass of petals, until a blossom seems to close to nightfall. All round, small lights begin to be lit in homes and on streets, and the ending day withdraws into night. A high moon brings the languid shadows of boats and shrines and people on the beach to clarity and emptiness.

Perhaps it is only the blankness of the blue that makes the villages and town a clutter. Perhaps it is the sea's cleanness that makes them squalid, and its expanse that makes people appear small-minded. The mathematical repetition of waves reaching infinity gives effort and relationship a messy quality, giving rise to comparison merely by existing. Its beauty can make men poor indeed, and are they courageous just in living by the sea? Is it the fisherman who has come to a full dignity by being there all his life, and by making his livelihood from the sea? Or is it the simple pilgrim who touches the foam with his fingers and gains closeness? Is it the maker of the temple, long dead, who lives on? Between the eroded niche and the broken seed, is a secret held a secret, a conquest made to remain unknown? Has the town become unconcerned, too loud? Are the tide-clipped conversations of beachcombers a testimony to a nearing? Does the nocturnal drunkard suppress that yearning? Is the sea futile, and how does it draw people to itself from afar? Can it repel? Does it conceal its fearsomeness in its greatness? Is the sea merely an emotion? Is it fundamentally only a thought? Is thought ever so beautiful? As fingers reach to touch it, are the ends of it that the eyes witness only imagined extremities? Is only what lies before one's eyes a reality and the rest a progression towards imagination? Is imagination at the periphery of reality, the cradle within which it rests? Are the furthest waves that fade to the right and to the left imagined? Does the sea rise from nowhere, like the water in the shrine? Is the source of the water one's heart? Is the source cool and deeply embedded under burning sands, and does it remain as invisible as the source of the wind, knowable only by the direction it takes? Is man the closed-door room where nothing stirs? One sees the sea, and then there is nothing. Then one sees that the blue becomes two ribbons of white as they touch land. One has to sit in time to know recurrence and to eradicate eternity. Time then becomes magical, as magical as the words of the priest are to the unknowing villager. Not all the centuries of adroitness can compel that simplicity to knowledge, nor all the myths and portents win that innocence. It is simplicity as yet free and untouched, it fades and becomes hesitant, but its moment is as yet real. The eyes see directly ahead of one, and those windswept fingers do not emerge from the corner of one's eyes. The eyes have come upon them whole, suddenly. There is only a shallow mystery in imagination, in those extremities from which ones thinks the real world is born, but the deeper mystery is before one, readymade. That mystery is simplest, like a cloth that is woven two ways, but is of one texture and melts into a single surface of no crisscrossing threads. Do the weft and the warp assume the texture of the sea? Can only the sourceless wind make it happen, or are the sources deep within the being of the water itself, to propel arithmetic and a repetition? Where is the individual in all of this? He becomes an entity that is negligible indeed in that vastness, yet does he exist because he has feeling? The quietest mystery is with the unknowing finger that upturns recognised balances and spreads a new reality before one, a reality of all things in constant upheaval underneath ordered textures; the joyous flutter of swifts and the mundane rumble of buses, the innocuous and explosive shouts of brawls. In a closed room incense curls and a pillar unfurls that in the open wind would only evaporate, leaving a sterile source, a futile ember aglow in daylight. Is the temple really an ember in the sun? Is that the message of art that has been rescued by a seed, burst into a million leaves that unravel finely stitched stones? There is a silence in the sea, and there is a silence that does not speak in the raucous bazaar, a silence that cannot speak on the stretch of no-man's land between a ghost town and a blue desert. There is silence too, when virgin rays strike the carved drummer at the temple summit. In an unknown corner of the world, an anonymous dawn weaves into a vast day, making a symphony out of itself, and the silence is forgotten and unable to be heard. The silence is gone in the drumming of the world and in its senseless thunder. Where there is compassion, it glimmers through inexplicable and inaccessible like a niche of lovers in far granite.

Two fisherwomen walk towards each other on the beach, carrying baskets on their heads. As soon as they come within shouting distance of each other, the exchange of words starts a flood of speech. When their paces come together, their baskets collide. Without either of them lifting the cheroots off their mouths, one woman lights her

31

own off the other's, all hands remaining on baskets overhead. After the quiet moment of lighting, they unhinge their baskets from each other and march off, both puffing and chattering in their own directions, without so much as turning around. And not once in the entire transaction have their eyes met.

To have a white sea, a grey beach, a black city; to have bright orange fish in the sea, to have golden crabs on the beach, and purple-skinned people in the city; to have black houses and black furniture, to have brown carpets and pink plants; to have green boats on the sea, and a blue sun in a crème sky; to have turquoise fingernails and white teeth and eyes; to have always the wind, never stillness; to have a sea whose foam never makes a sound, whose spray never evaporates but is silver and sprinkles like ball bearings on the beach; to drink fluorescent coloured drinks, to eat silver and copper and gold food; to have flowers and sunsets like the rainbow; to have gentle music in the city, and silence by the shore.

The sand burns in the noon, and as one walks, pulling the bicycle through the dunes, the grains flick over one's feet like so many sparks, scalding momentarily. The sea lies in the distance, a relentless blue, and as the tide recedes, it leaves a hard sandy stretch upon which one can easily ride, a road smoother than those of the town. One has taken almost nothing along except the bag of cakes and cigarettes and a little bit of money. The sun is strong in the cloudless sky, and one wishes one had brought a cap too.

The beach is firm and flat and one speeds past the empty town houses to the fishing village. There are groups on the beach, fetching boats and nets from the water, laying out fish on the ground and putting away the haul into various baskets. There are always children, romping in the foam. The bicycle makes their eyes light up and they break out in smiles and wave their arms. One does not stop except where the sand is too soft and where the wheels do not pull. The village is large and sprawls for a few kilometres, and as one looks ahead, one sees where the dark figures of people and the brown roofs end, and the emptiness of the beach begins. It curves behind a casuarina forest and disappears against the water that becomes a monochromatic glare on the horizon. One races, straining at the pedals, enjoying the whir of wheels on the even floor, and soon one passes the village.

The beach empties suddenly, and apart from the tiny, wobbling silhouettes of a couple of fishermen in the distance, there is nothing upon which the eyes can focus. A few birds seem to materialise from stark, windy air, coming into sight and disappearing plainly, leaving shrieks that dissolve into the rumble of the tide. In the emptiness the sun strengthens and the wind sharpens, the sensation of speeding becomes clearer, and one flies, joyous of momentum.

A bushy jungle grows to the edge of the beach and is bordered with a shaky stile made of twigs and dried palm leaves. The sands are no longer dappled with footprints. They have been smoothened by the wind that has left ripples that shine darkly, revealing ribs of wet sand under dry dust. Jellyfish has been swept ashore and litter the sand like white buttons with deep blue rings, and embedded among them are shells as tiny as bird claws. A clump of blue string lies among the rubble, and there is the tatter of a net that has also been washed up, vestiges of civilisation on the deserted sand. As one speeds, the sea arrives at uniformity on the right side, and little things on the beach catch one's interest. In the distance are a few dark objects, and one wonders whether they will become people as one moves closer, or whether they will remain immobile like pieces of driftwood or boulders. The beach continues past the forest to a broad bay that ends in another forest of higher trees. On coming nearer, the gnarled trunks of trees appear, and a few stumps lie half-covered in the sand, corpses shocked white over years of abandonment to sun and wind. Against the air current, three giant gulls fly and shriek, alighting on the wet ground among throngs of sandpipers; then they glide low on the waves and go further down the beach. One does not stop, but drives on, propelled by something behind one or by the wind or the sound of breakers. A little ahead is a small mound of sand, and a blue basket lies by its side, motionless in the wind and strange on the sands where no feet have seemed to tread. There is a rivulet at the edge of trees, lapping gently on the thundering waves as it fans out to sea. Getting off the bicycle and wiping the sweat off one's brow, yet not looking back to the expanse one has traveled, one checks the depth of the water. One decides to wade through, pulling the bicycle along. The water is cool on one's feet and reaches the ankles, and one is tempted to drink. The banks of the rivulet have been sliced away by the motion of the water, and halfway across, the sandbed softens underneath one and the bicycle becomes hard to pull. Soon past the water, looking back, one sees how tiny the rivulet really has been. Further behind, one has left a thin track that vanishes in the distance. Is imagination really in the distance and not at the periphery of one's sight? The sea fades on one side, and the sand on the other side does as well. That which is directly in front dims too, and then, in brisk attention, one wipes the sand clinging to the feet, and climbs on the seat again, looking ahead, wondering about the dark blobs far away. A feeling of emptiness sweeps momentarily over one; it is not entirely pleasant because it contains a glimmer of aloneness. The moment of rest from driving onward has revealed one's isolation upon a vast beach by an unpeopled land and a vacant sea. One feels happy at moving again and in being preoccupied at the wheel.

The sea recedes from one's attention, the beach upon which one races obscures, and the sky becomes nonexistent. Perhaps it is necessary to have the black blurs to concentrate upon and to make for curiosity. Do they save one from a fearful introspection? The salts that have settled on the face burn at the beard, and lips taste salty. The wind wipes away sweat as one drives on. The sun is behind one, throwing a clean shadow of the bicycle a little ahead, showing that the bag behind one is secure. One has done perhaps twenty-five kilometres on the beach. One is not exhausted, but one thinks to walk a bit and carry the bicycle on one's side. The black blurs come closer, three fisherwomen. They have probably come from villages that lie not far inland, although no settlement can be seen from the beach. In passing them, one sees perplexity written all over their faces. One smiles back at them, feeling only a relief at having chanced across humanity. The plastic bucket, the piece of wood with the nail in it, the blue string and the net has not misled one; they have become queer totems. The fisherwomen are silent; secretly, one wishes for voices.

There are sands again, the sound of the tide, the bare sky, the flight of a lonely seagull. On the bicycle again, one tosses the cigarette stub to the water. The tide is low and skims out very broad on the horizontal sand, a thin rim of suds rolls and is sucked in as water withdraws into the vast blue body. The rolling stub goes invisibly into a sea that begins to display its strangeness and mystery in open daylight.

Once again the ride seems uneventful. There is sea to one side, and sand to the other, sloping upward so that no land is visible beyond it, but only sky. Looking down at one's shadow and occasionally glancing back, one sees the string that the wheels draw over the beach. The sands must be endless; in the furthest corner they become a misty blur, the colours of breakers merge with ground and sky that are also of the same shapeless texture. There are always multiple views to anything because the mind is anchored to the eyes in ways both subtle and strong. Are there innumerable threads that bind it, or is there a singular umbilical cord, like the track that is being spider-spun behind? Is the track necessary, does the uncharted territory ahead compel it to be spun? Is the track a trophy for its maker, a gift for someone who might wish to follow? Does the beach have to be covered merely because it exists? Is the sea something beyond mere strangeness and mystery? Does it obliterate the track in the same way that it swallows the cigarette stub? Or can it become benevolent and gnaw at it slowly, like the driftwood that lies charred by the spray? Is that its message? And the temple that lies miles ahead, should it not be there at all as a goal? Is it clear now that the entire journey is in the going, and does the knowledge that a temple rests by the sands destroy a message in this arduous and lonely moving onward? Is it the boredom and austerity of one's surrounding that provokes the mind to ramble inward? Does it thereby make for a retreat that is intricate and fascinating to a glowing world that is somehow created by the experience of the body? Is the mind the glittering pearl set in the oyster, and is the seabed necessary to the pearl? Or can only the oyster be conscious of the seabed in order to let the pearl have life? Which is the most precious of the three, are they all at a par?

Alone on a bicycle as one has never known before, the frailty of oneself has still to make an impression upon oneself. One has been too busy moving on, breathing heavily while straining at the paddles. Physical exhaustion preoccupies one, blocking the imagining mind as it veers time and again to dangerous thoughts, bringing it to a balance by the simple act of seeing. As the mind enters fearful worlds of its own making, the world around one recedes. Those worlds to which it has access bring an added peril because one cannot react to the real dangers one is exposed to on the boundless desert. One speeds on a tightrope track made by oneself on a no-man's land. One only realizes when one gets off the bicycle how alone one really is. The actual situation retreats when one welcomes thoughts in whose harmony the experience becomes livable and even alluring. Yet of what use is that gain if what has become alluring does not also reveal its truth in being exactly what it is? That is a trick or a miracle that only a mind with a heart can perform. For that to happen, there can be no awareness of the linear and effortless pushing under wheels. The track has to be abandoned for the thoughts to survive whole, and that is a blessing that never comes.

Instead, ahead of one, the sands curve inward and a broad river behind the sands rolls to the sea, quieter than the waves against which it is annihilated. One is struck by the beauty of the river and at its deep azure that spreads and flattens into foam and is gone. Perhaps it is not possible to cross it in the same way one did with the earlier rivulet. Sand has been carved away as the river makes its delta. The clean edges are frayed and rippled as if hesitantly; the river has known how much to take and the beach how much to give. Beyond, the river swings sharply in a hairpin bend; the sand mounts several feet at the conical point in its course, at the last curve before it reaches the sea. An old thatch hut is perched on the mound, a ruin that the fishermen maybe rarely use.

Ahead, past the broad delta, are four figures on the far side of the river, and they are colourful specks dilating in the wind. They have probably been able to wade across, although it seems several hundred feet wide at the place where the river meets the waves. How can one carry oneself and the bicycle as well? Cupping one's hands over the mouth, one shouts out, and shouts again. There is no answer, no speck stops in its pace. One cannot be heard. Although the distance is not too great, the roar of the waves muffles the shrillest cry. Even the giant gulls that float over the foam cannot be heard too far. The space is too open and too flat, and is overtaken by winds. One's throat is dry and grains of salt have accumulated on the face and neck. The wind has dried all perspiration in the strong afternoon sun, and one's head pounds. One fetches a cake and eats it, thankful for its moist sweetness. One is thirsty but one resists the river water. One is alone. Is one alone merely for having spotted people?

The bicycle on the sand seems suddenly frail, so small that one wonders how it has been able to get one to this veritable edge of nowhere at all. It glitters chrome in the sun and appears immensely lonely, an alien on the beach. One looks back to the river and its clear blue water, following its gentle lapping to the huge thunder of the sea. How simply it gives itself, like a line of poetry flowing into the harsh light of prose. It is as if the river stretches out, relaxes before its end, and in a silence is consumed by the wild roar, in peace to anger and to tyranny. Its sweetness is swept over by acrid salts, its clarity to froth and mud, and its mirror-still surface is eaten in a turbulent mist.

The ruin hut has darkened and become brittle in the sun and wind as witness to a timeless sacrifice and ritual. There is no fear in the contemplation nature induces, and it is only the vanishing specks that remind one of time and the world. Is one a hermit who belongs to the abandoned hut? Would it shield one against the chill of night if one has to stay, or is it infested with serpents? For a moment one remembers the dead snake one has passed a few kilometers behind, and one shudders. The innocent façade of the hut makes one forget all that, and, walking towards it, the broad sweep of the river against the land overtakes one's thoughts.

It is green on the other bank, it is as if the river has ignored one side but given plenty to the other. The terrain is flat and bushy and ends in a lush forest of palm trees. Between green hillocks and thick brush are huts that jut skyward. On a hill stands a whitewashed temple that is hidden by trees overlooking the river below. Small paths lead to the temple and are overgrown with roots that serve as footholds. One can discern details of windows and the thickets that border them. The temple is deserted at this hour. There is no one about, and yet warmth emanates from the lonely hamlet. One is unable to reach it, but just a glimpse from the sandy shore chases away dark thoughts. Now the loneliness that comes is of another kind; one feels an affinity with the hut on the mound and the vast blue expanse behind it. The hamlet basking in the sun on the other shore would remain unknown to one; it can belong only to the coloured speck figures that walked away or to the hidden people living near the shrine. Perhaps because there is suddenly a relationship with humanity and civilization, the only awareness that emerges is of one's inherent isolation. There is no antagonism, only a lack of any contact, and that solitude becomes both real and symbolic. It is not of oneself that it speaks, it is of all men, and one only happens to be there at the time to know it. The inside becomes the outside. Is it for this knowledge that one has traveled so far? The temple on the shore that lies many kilometers beyond the river delta had been a destination, yet in seeing an inaccessible and unexpected shrine on the other bank, has a previous goal been removed and set aright? Can one make a goal of something one only chances upon? Is that the lesson? Isolation gives way to helplessness, and further up the river there are long dark boats at rest; very far away there are thin black figures of fishermen. One glances quickly and returns to fetch the bicycle. They can never hear from where one stands, although the rise in sand blocks sea sounds. One would have to drag the bicycle through the thick sand to a point opposite the boats and hope that the fishermen would spot the shine on the bicycle. They may then bring the boats to the deserted shore and carry one across the river to reach the green bank. One runs through the heavy sand, panting for breath. The head reels with the burning sun.

The river is deep azure and tranquil, the rising sand shields the sea from view, and the land has a serenity apart from the harsh openness of the beach. The huts are peaceful and nestle under palm trees, and figures by the water have slow movements, as if they live without the knowledge of the sea and its relentless toil. There is no constant wind upon the bank as there is on the beach, the air is still, and the sun breaks on the ground in a pitiless and silent fury. The sands scorch through the shoes and the bicycle seems heavier as one tugs it through soft sand. Perhaps the chrome of spokes and handlebars will glint in the direction of the figures, and they will notice one's presence.

The sand slopes downward to the edge of the river, and, pushing oneself along it, one finds that it is easier to negotiate than hard ground. The figures are still a few kilometers away, and one starts to trudge back over the incline, hoping that one's silhouette is visible against the sky. One leaves the bicycle on the sand where it assumes the look of a forsaken carcass, and one walks empty-handed to the riverside, shouting and waving to the figures. It is hopeless. They seem not to even raise their eyes, and continue to potter among their boats as if no outsider exists.

Sweat breaks out on one in the still hot air, and one smudges one's face feverishly. They do not care, even if they have seen, and there will be no boat to cross the river. The afternoon sun is lowing in the sky, the day is wearing on, and one worries about being stranded on the forlorn stretch of sand. If evening comes and finds one still waving one's arms in vain, one would not be able to even consider riding back to the fisher's village that is so far away. One would have to endure the night in the ruin hut- but there are only two cakes left. There is thirst and one does not dare to drink from the river. The hot dry sands and the sun do nothing to mitigate one's dilemma. One has to act fast. If one decides to stay, there is time to swim in the river at leisure and hope for help. But if one wants to reach town, one is already short of time, and the tide may already have risen, making the ride impossible upon the sand. There will be no help from those innocuous figures; it is they, ironically, who are isolated, and give the impression of not wanting to be disturbed by strangers. Their silence and negligence seem hostile, and one feels a surge of remorse and fear shoot through one intermingled with an indescribable feeling of futility and sadness.

"I am understanding something that has never been understood before."

Frenetically, one flies back in the direction of the bicycle, and then, carrying it, one makes for the beach. The sea lurches ahead, and for all its fury, still gives solace. The familiar breeze brushes against clothes and brow and soon makes one forget the hamlet, those deaf and mute silhouettes with whom one had tried to speak, of whom one had had need, and who one had tried to love. The footsteps left behind have loneliness in their imprint that the night tide will erase. Have there been other strangers in this land before? The sea will not reveal that. Perhaps the attitude of the fisher folk tells something even in its silent unconcern. Speeding on the bicycle, finding that one's body is breaking with exhaustion, and the wind difficult to drive against, one wonders whether one is able to care for these strange figures encountered beyond the river. They are gone, and one is alone again, but one is so much more spent than one was at noon. With the tide rising threateningly comes nervousness. There are parts of the single bicycle track that still remain; other parts have been erased by the waves, like a string broken in many places. Is one wrong in feeling that the track is really the heart that has been torn into countless shreds? The lonely ride, the sea of anger, the pitiless sun, the hostile sand and the heartbreaking callousness of strangers: was there only labour and futility, was that the sole adventure? The danger of the rising tide, the oncoming chill of night, the hiss of snakes and the calls of wild animals, the incapacity of tired limbs and a parched throat that cannot permit tears: is this all there is? The repetition of a journey on an old track, the humiliation of not being able to wade through the river, of a forced return: who knew what more this desert held back within its arid vastness? Who knew what a clash of two deserts, the golden and the blue, could conjure against a vapid sky?

The sea ahead breaks into feverish foam that is robbed of any colour. The sun gives it sheen of mother-of-pearl, and the air lends it the aura of mist. There seems to be no horizon but only a colourless vapour. One looks ahead and below to find torn bits of track in order to judge the mounting tide. The wind then takes on a frightening rancour, a power that one will consistently have to fight in going the direction of the town. Too soon, the sun will set and darkness rule the desert, effacing the lines between land and water. One will be trapped on a diminishing strip that moves with the rushing tide to its quotidian extinction.

From now, it is an obsessive journey backwards, the throat gasping and dry, the tide rising. There is only the ache of return, and fatigue. Passing a few groups of fishermen, one asks where one might get water to drink. They do not seem to understand, and when one gestures, cupping hand over mouth, they nod: there is none. Legs have not been able to take the strain of ploughing through hard sand any longer, and one has to walk at intervals, then mount the bicycle and ride on.

The waves leave a rim of salt; the burning sands singe the water on one's brow instantaneously. One wipes it away and it grates against the residue of salt on one's neck. One walks along the surf and spots tiny blue shells on the sand. Halting for one nervous moment, one picks them up. They are as tiny as grains of rice and are a startling blue, and perhaps that is the reason one notices them at all. They are fragile, a few crumble at the touch; with care, one puts them away into the matchbox.

One drives on as before, no more the carefree despite the treasure the fierce sea has tossed one's way. One wades through the rivulet again, and there is relief at being able to measure the distance remaining to cover. A burden seems to lift as one gets to the other side, and one looks back for just an instant, only to see that the tide has advanced considerably since noon.

As the sun dips behind trees and the colours of sand and sea merge into grey, one sees the settlements not far away, dark forms against the lowering sky, spiked in places by triangle cloths stitched on bamboo poles. One lessens one's pace, and gets off the bicycle to walk. One's sore feet are lapped by waves.

Looking behind, one can scarcely discern land from sea. There is a tireless breathing of the tide, a fearful and unconquerable gush of sound that freezes into darkness, and then grows out of it mercilessly.

There have been fast winds that night and there has been rain. There has been the threat of a cyclone from the sea, and one has feared for the fishermen's huts that may have been blown away, plundered painlessly by the elements.

All night, winds rage.

In the morning, the air is calm; the sun shines benign like the smile of a newborn infant. The wild winds have swept the sand over piles of ropes and nets, over boats, over the spring shrine, so that everything looks like a half-buried, half-found treasure. The sands that are always mottled by footprints are now like a sheet without a single crease, virginal and silent.

An Old Citadel

An Old Citadel

Steps lead through ruined walls to the summit of the hill, past broken buildings within the fort. One passes bazaars, enters an enormous archway after taking a sweeping turn of the road, and moves up through hallways to open ground and bushy paths. There are glimpses of the sprawling city below.

Boulders jut out from the stone walls as if ready to tumble down, and the sound of traffic comes up with the wind. Dark rooms are isolated in their state of ruination. Their granite walls have the musty smell peculiar to such places. The sunshine outside, by contrast, is brilliant. One mounts the wide and tattered staircases under the sky, taking each broken stone in one's stride carefully. It is as if one were ascending a monochrome in which the shades become clearer and airier as one goes further. The countryside is only partially green and is boulder-studded. Hillocks rise out of the undulating land like brown-grey amphibians and melt into the haze. The new buildings are tiny glowing cubes.

All that remains of the fort is a hill of broken walls, making for a fascinating walk through structures perched strangely at angles with no apparent plan. Higher up, there is a mosque amid stone courtyards, and is well preserved, but lies unused. The view of the city becomes more spectacular. Grasses and bushes grow wild through stones and cracks in floors. In the growing distance below, a wisp of lake shimmers, hidden partly by grey hillocks. Boulders add much atmosphere to the walls that must have once stood upright. The years have transformed the hill, and given it a charm it could not have had when newly built and lived in.

One comes completely unawares to a temple that has been hidden from view. After all the blacks and browns of stones, colour assaults one. There is yellow and blue under the weird rock that has a bright Om painted upon it, under the double triangle of red flag that flutters in the breeze. A young pundit looks on quietly. A tiny shrine behind the main temple has just about been squeezed under the whitewashed boulder, and is dedicated to Durga. It is indeed a stunning little monument and much more inspired than the main temple, set as it is on a deserted hill with its own enclosure and sunken courtyard, steps and tree. The boulder towers high above the door of the shrine that is festooned with dry leaves and is painted as brightly as possible. These two shrines, tucked away under a stone that resembles the form of Nandi, are delightful architectural objects, aglow in a setting of drab browns, shiny under the matte whitewash of rocks. One has to enter a tiny doorway to receive the blessings of the goddess ensconced under a convex rock ceiling. There is scarcely room enough for the pundit to squat.

One continues further up to the durbar halls that form the highest structure on the hill. They have been resuscitated and plastered in the modern manner, and have in fact become ruined ruins. A steep and narrow staircase leads to the terrace and to the very pinnacle of the fort from where a small open-air pavilion affords a magnificent view of the city. One sees how the city has extended itself right up to the ramparts, for there are modern buildings among the boulder-strewn countryside.

Then, descending a perfect staircase that comes straight down the hill, one turns away from the monuments. One skirts high walls to other palaces that are laid out at a lower level. Enormous archways let in shafts of light as if the rock floors belonged to a theatre or a cathedral, and light corridors and passageways unexpectedly. Then one is out again under the sky, suddenly among roofless ruins that spread for hundreds of yards between grasses and thorny bushes. One walks through giant corridors and past broken walls to emerge on the bright modern-day bazaar and tiny, noisy streets. One suddenly realizes how silent the visit to the fort has been. Passing slum villages, one comes to the tombs of kings long dead in gardens of dry grass and shady trees. There are five or six monuments with curious onion-like domes. The stark and geometric tombstones are of black granite, solitary in their empty rooms that are framed in archways. They are better preserved than the fort although they date from the same period four centuries ago.

One has descended to the level of the city, but the enormity of the fort is still with one and dominates the view from the tombs. One looks up to it and imagines how it must once have been a bustling and opulent township, now merely a tattered and torn skeleton. Its unique ambience is evaporating as the city advances behind the hill. Once it must have been a lonely and inaccessible citadel, well protected from enemy and intruder by its height and self-sufficiency, with its unique drainage system, water tanks and the many necessary facilities it provided for civic life to thrive independently.

Birds wheel in a cyan sky. There is no longer loneliness among the ruins because they are so frequented. Yet they evoke a grandeur and lofty aloofness that is all too alien in today's world.

The Lure of Faraway Islands

The Lure of Faraway Islands

Watching only water and sky and a timeless vastness all round brings about a peacefulness, cleanness and simplicity. One is what one sees. If one lives in the city, one sees only ambition and greed and envy, and one escapes into art and culture, but it only brings about a cultivation and an outer refinement. When one sees nature and is within it, then there is openness towards simplicity. A lifetime of that kind of seeing makes for a fine human being.

A spray is intermittent and rises with the breeze. The waves are chopped; they are little white waves throughout the water surface that heaves, stretching as far as the eyes can see. There are curls of waves and the textures of more waves on what is already there, so that one sees myriad patterns. The water is dark blue. The sun behind swiftly moving clouds creates islands of light that glitter on the surface, and are soon lost when the sun comes into the clear again, making a path of molten metal instead. There are no birds, only a light and vastness that is matched by the largeness of the sea. The breeze is now strong, now gentle. People onboard throw paper to the wind, and the flutter of scraps rises high above the ship and travels far out to sea. There is music, there are voices around one, but they do not disturb. A little away from all this, on a bench on deck, there is only the murmur of the water and wind and sounds of the vibrating ship. One can sit for hours with eyes open, scarcely remembering to blink, and one becomes two vast elements. One becomes that simplicity in watching, and then, coming down to crowded decks, one is surrounded with people burdened with their minds, their wants and boredom.

He lives somewhere on the islands along with the rest of his tribe, and his laughter has only his heart in it and possesses a rare purity. Perhaps only a saint could have that laughter, spontaneous, full, and emanating from the source of all strength of spirit. The laughter of the aboriginal is fragile and can be shattered with the slightest contact with modernity. It took the anthropologists five days to establish a rapport with them, because they would run into the forests upon sighting the intruders. They inched closer to the inhabitants at last, and when they handed them a pouch of tobacco, they laughed. The anthropologists had never heard that kind of laughter before. But slowly, with more and more temptations from the cities, that laughter will vanish. The laughter of the saint cannot diminish because he laughs within the world. Yet what difference does it make? That kind of laughter exists, whether it is there in the soul of an island, or in the heart of a city. It is the very essence of humanity, and both ways are precious: one by knowing the world and by retaining one's essential being, and the other in merely being. Can there be communication with the wild and free man, having the city in one's head and the world in one's bones? Perhaps only one who is truly simple can laugh in complete communion with the aboriginal. The freedom that one is obliterates the fact that one is wild or tamed; there is only freedom. The free need protection, and yet, in that very act, one destroys. Yet so what if they become extinct? Perhaps the only way left is to live within the world and retain simplicity, knowing both the place of nature and that of the mind.

The sunset is swift, and the sky lights up red as the sun goes behind the trail of clouds and into the sea. The night sea is black, and one can still feel its heaving body although one no longer sees it. The sky is dark and incandescent and bright with stars. The clouds are black, dull and very solid, diagonal in their movement from the horizon onwards. A veil of clouds obscures the line between sea and sky. One can sit engulfed in darkness all night, not wishing for the dawn.

It rains in the morning, and by the afternoon, one passes small islands and nears the port. The islands are rich green, studded each inch with trees and grass so that no soil is visible. They rise like young hills from the water; here and there are white streaks of sand that are untouched. The sky is black in one part and golden in another. The water is all a shimmering blue, and the ship floats gently into port, passing a few small fishing boats at sunset. Houses nestle under trees in the low-lying hillocks along the island. There are layers of colour on the land, deep green becoming grey and blue as they recede into the distance under a cloudy sky.

There is a golden cove between rocks next to a quarry, a half-circle of white sand and intensely blue water. The waves are gentle and the sky seems even bluer. The beach is hidden between two hills that are rich green. Palm trees sway in the breeze; a small rocky island in the water has a solitary dead tree upon it. People come to bathe or lie in the sun, and they are small against the waves and curve of land. Shell animals crawl on the beach, leaving pinhead-size trails as they move. A tiny crab makes perfect balls of sand under its body and tosses them up. There are countless balls around crab holes laid out centrifugally. A small white puppy wags his tail at the slightest provocation. A little fishing boat brings in a haul of small silver fish and villagers gather round the catch. There are a few poor thatch huts on the rocks where they live, and behind them is the quarry where a few labourers hack stones in the shade of trucks. The hillocks behind are thick with vegetation. Clouds gather and fleet by fast, making shady and sunny patterns on the sand. The surf splashes white on rocks. Tiny shell animals in the cracks of rocks try not to be swept by the small waves. By the water's edge where the surf breaks, hundreds of green crabs scurry about or sun themselves.

It rains. A grey parallelogram descends from a cloud, slanting into the water, and the sea turns green. Fishermen gather a large net. The rain leaves the beach speckled and dark. Grey clouds trail the sky, and the fishermen pull in a net. Elsewhere, others sort out fish on sand. There are people about, but one is not aware of time. Idleness becomes encased in a halo.

The roads in the town are never straight, but wind up and down around verdant hillocks, and are rainwashed eight months of the year. The main bazaar is small and goes uphill and is a delight to visit in the clean afternoon sunshine. Shops seem to jostle each other for space and sell countless things. There are scruffy restaurants, juice stalls, sweet and teashops. Hundreds of people descend steps from a cinema where a show has just given over. Crowds are not oppressive. The people in buses are dark and simpler than town folk.

A road clings low to the sea, winding through green hillocks of meadows dotted with palm and other trees, and leads to the beach. Everything on the way reflects the morning light. Water scintillates, the leaves of palm trees are glossy and even the breeze seems to waft light. Dark rocks by the edge of water are glistening and the line of sea is poker straight. The strata of rocks can be seen under the water, eroded in places, but retaining a rectangular form. The water is like a silver lame, and further up the coast, fishermen are pulling at a rope in the sea, and they are dark and fine.

The bus goes through lush forests and comes down to the seaside only to wind up again into the trees. Waves break upon reefs a way into the water, and the sea is tremendously blue. Large trees reach to the very edge of the water. In places, the sea has claimed trees, and they lie there dead and bleached, exposing root and branch and taking sinister forms. There are tiny hutments in the forest. One tree is cruelly upturned in the water and its enormous tangle of roots has stones embedded in it.

The road leads to a tranquil bay. Islands on the other side are grey-green and the water in between is flat and rippled and in all shades of blue under the influence of gathering rain clouds. Mangroves grow in the shallow water, propped on their roots as if on stilts. Three boats rock gently in the limpid water. The clouds play endlessly with light upon green hills and set the water shimmering in countless hues. One boat twirls ever so slowly in the ripples, the very picture of solitude against the still hills and the calm lake-like sea and silent, full sky.

The people smile at each other at the slightest invitation and they laugh with each other as they go about their chores. They are unhurried and one can learn how to take time over small things from them. Their happiness seems the norm and an ordinary thing. They are interested in one, but not inquisitive. Their minds are not preoccupied and there is an air of ease about their activities. They are poor but live within their means and do not seem to want any more. They find it difficult to get by, but accept it in their stride. Nothing seems to bother them, and so they go through their days in a certain calmness. They are not too exposed to the temptations of the big world. They live within a beautiful environment, and although they may be largely unaware of that, they are nevertheless affected by the serenity it induces in their lives. The mainland does hold great attraction for them, but most of them will never be able to afford a visit there. Thus it is put out of their minds, and life on the islands carries on peacefully. If one has eyes to see it, the happiness is indeed there, in the way they talk to each other and in the manner in which they go about the most mundane tasks. A boy makes tea, paan, dispenses medicine to young children and gives them advice as well, all with buoyancy in his voice. The people are neither proud not humble, and certainly do not grope or want to achieve anything that is unnecessary to their lives. Their preoccupations end with finding enough to eat, a roof over their heads, keeping in moderately good health, and in not having insurmountable problems. They do not look beyond that; if they do not use their minds, at least they do not misuse them, as most of humanity tends to do. The expression "no problems" would apply to them, and that implies a lack of awareness of problems also, and assuming no responsibility for the state of the world as it is. They are indeed the product of the calmness of faraway places, not under the influence of any persuasion that so often goes wrong and causes turmoil. There must be temples and churches, but the people seem unconcerned by them. They do not desire happiness; they are that happiness itself. The moment they start wanting, a certain quality will disappear. They seem unique and yet in many ways are like everyone else. Part of the reason they are such is because they are not overcrowded into little spaces; there is always the openness of water, the abundance of nature. There is always greenery around their little shacks, no matter how humble they may be. Money has not brought about a loud garishness and perhaps it will never be there to do so. In the very ordinariness of things, there is charm. One has but to venture a kilometre out of town to be in deep forests. The roads that wind through the countryside may have one or two trucks upon them, but no one walking on the path. Further inland, the roads stop. The local people are not too concerned about receiving fresh produce from the mainland, although fresh fruit and vegetables are not usually available on the island. It is unimaginable that they treat these commodities as luxuries, and yet they make do with so little. It does not diminish their joy.

The forests come right down to the sea in every shade of green. There is not a square inch of ground left: saplings have taken everything up. There are huts in the village, possibly the humblest that are imaginable, and yet they are clean. They are not bunched together but are scattered over the countryside. People harvest radishes, using two bullocks and ploughshares to till the fields. The few birds one sights are bright and colourful. Roads lead past a small jetty. The water here is placid and reflects the clear sky. Empty boats rock gently on tiny waves. There are a few swifts, a couple of dogs chase each other in abandon, and an old fisherman washes a boat further ahead. There are green islands into the water that shimmers grey in the afternoon sun. Along the sand banks, there is an enormous quantity of fallen trees, bleached cadavers that have idled there for centuries. These gnarled and twisted forms continue up to the narrow beach, and there, in sheer contrast to the lush countryside, a scene of sudden desolation and complete destruction confronts one. Water, wind and sun have conspired to lay a land waste. Trees have fallen into the water by the hundreds. It is almost as if the water has twisted them, branches, roots and upturned trunks, and tortured them into a new metamorphosis. An entire forest that grew too close to water was vanquished. For kilometers along the beach, these cadavers lie, black, white and colourless. They shine in parts that have been completely worn away and the bark has turned grey and hangs in patches on some trunks in a great variety of textures. Yet only a few yards away, bushes are green and luxuriant, and trees grow with thick shiny leaves, tall trees are straight. The forest begins suddenly and is immediately thick. There is no free ground. Beyond, palm tree plantations continue up to the hillocks. Here on the narrow beach even the rocks are being eroded and the shallow stones are turning to grit and mixing in with the coral that has been rounded by so many years of exposure to the elements. The water is in all shades of blue and the waves are tiny. The line of sea is clean against the sky and islands are grey but darken to black the nearer they are. Many trees have straight long trunks and at their extremities have clumps of roots that have pulled up mud and stones, making dark knots against the stark and over lit sky. On many of the trees, branches have sprouted leaves; weed and grasses grow on the dead wood as if to reassure one of the profusion of life even here. Small boats lie on the sand, not too different to the cadavers of trees that surround them. They have lain many years and are unusable, but there, into the water, a boat rocks upon waves. A little way behind on the beach, there is a mud path. It is a wild promenade over wind bent grasses and under leafy bushes and trees. The contrast of abundant life and sudden annihilation is strange to chance upon, and the bright sea beyond this narrow strip seems indifferent to it. It heaves and breathes and is alive and is a thing apart from both abundance and desolation, and therefore evokes eternity.

A Light on the Shore

A Light on the Shore

The sky is overcast and the sea is rough; seagulls are poised on berm and black sand is golden underneath. Two rock temples on the shore are triangles in the distance. As one nears them, one ascends steps to enter the courtyard of sand that is railed in by a low wall. The walls are lined with Nandis and most of them face one direction. The pagodas stand in the middle of the courtyard. Granite has been ravaged by the elements for centuries so that the forms of figures upon the gopurams have been eaten away, and the rock looks more like toffee than the stern granite so abundant here. Gods and demons that guard the temples on the outside and who are ensconced in the square panels within have completely lost their features, and occasionally also their limbs and torsos, not at the hands of vandals, but to salt spray. The wind and sea have gouged out huge fissures into the rock and given it strangeness and grandeur so that these forms seem not to belong to a real world but rather to one of dreams. They are from a realm where the mind is clouded and overtaken in the haze of a beautiful vision where forms emerge and recede faintly. The elements have bestowed immense beauty on the manmade facades by accentuating their austerity and bringing them closer to a magical world. Behind the browns of granite the sea rages grey and waves unfurl long and white. There once stood seven pagodas, and to protect the remaining two monuments, huge boulders have been brought upon the sand, creating a formidable shield from the sea. The smaller temple has a cubic cell with a black granite sculpture of Shiva and Parvati that is in good condition. Before it, in a hole dug out into the stone lie coins left by pilgrims and the light through the door gives them sheen. The narrow open passageway leads to the back of the temple. In a rectangular cell lies a sleeping Vishnu, his magnificent body nearly cramped into the length of the cell. Above him, a small square window lets in light. It is like coming upon a secret that has lain dormant since time immemorial, the god so serene and yet so worn away. The larger spire has a black and polished lingam that is angular and broken on top; behind it rest another Shiva and Parvati in brown stone. There are barely two uneven steps to where the lingam stands glinting in the environment of brown. There is the unmistakable smell of bats, almost like incense that grew into the granite over a period of time. In the simplicity and unornamented presence of the temple complex, that strong fragrance assumes a mystical power. The shapes of stones on the walls and those rising on the tapering spires are as deformed as bones, having been whittled away in the sun. The temples rise merely thirty feet and yet evoke a magnificence that much larger buildings fail to do. The modesty of these shore temples is touching and takes one unawares. Yet they alone have had the strength to withstand thirteen hundred years of salt spray and tide. The once ornate facades are vastly eroded, yet the devotion of their makers to Shiva and Vishnu ring clear and unimpeded to this day. Each tier of ruined rock bears witness to the purity of emotion of a people for their gods. This morning, as perhaps even a thousand years ago, the sleeping Vishnu is bedecked in flowers from the village. As he lies in his enclosure of glowing darkness agelessly asleep, a moment's offering of blossoms speaks too, among the waves, of the eternity of both temple art and humble worshipper. Outside, a gentle pradakshinapath is adorned by a wall of magnificent and crumbled Nandis and uplifts one with each silent step that is taken. Whenever night fell, ever so long ago, a lamp stood always lit in the garbagriha of Shiva. The calm flame served as unwavering beacon to ancient seafarers. It was a guide and assurance of their god and enhanced the beauty of the temple and bound a people closer to their creator. One does not need enormity in order to praise God, the stones say, one needs but purity.

The town is behind the narrow road that leads to the tiny bazaar. In a large temple tank filled with flowering hyacinth and green rubbery leaves, old shaven-headed men bathe and dry out their lungis. Among the trees much further on, is an enormous rock with the face of a tiger carved upon it. Monsters and minor gods are arranged around a cubicle that has been cut into the rock to form a cave for meditation. Yesterday's rain has collected into a shallow rectangular pool before the cave, reflecting sky and trees and rocks. There is tranquility in the silence. Over a thousand years ago, this was the venue for music festivals. Coming upon it on a quiet afternoon, shielded from the sound of the sea, it has an otherworldly beauty.

The five rathas, in another part of the town, are charming when taken together in their special enclosure, although each one represents a unique monolithic style of carving. One looks like a thatch hut, another like a Buddhist vihara, a third like a larger temple; another stands isolated with a single cell carved into it and is different in character. There is a carved lion and an elephant on the grounds, and behind the row of four rathas, a squatting Nandi is gigantic and unadorned. The rock protrudes from the floor in places, untouched and uncarved. It seems almost easy to see how carvers went to work on the boulders that lay strewn in the countryside. Many sculptures are incomplete and closely resemble the rocks that lie about. It heightens the charm of the complex and breathes another vitality into it. Their surfaces bear chisel marks, the ridges appear like the lines on one's thumb. The transition from raw rock to polished stone can be seen in all its stages, standing there together in one frozen moment. It is not time that has withered the rathas, it is the hand of the sculptor that stood still, as if whimsically or under an angelic spell. In the village further down the road, the living generation of sculptors fashion newer gods and demons, their chisels tinkering into the silent morning. It is these musical sounds one finds all along the street, rising above the occasional car going past, or the wandering herds of goats and cows with bells around their necks, or the tinkle of bicycle bells.

The hill around the lighthouse has several caves, some of which are ornately carved with scenes of gods and goddesses. It is a pleasant walk among boulders and through dense forest. A huge rock perched upon a rocky slope is called Krishna's Butterball, and one wonders how it reached there. One gets a charming view of the surrounding fields, hills and river from a small shrine upon the highest rocks. Two cells are humane and touching in their portrayal of cowherds and animals. Nearby is a large bas-relief upon a boulder that is a magnificent collection of gods, goddesses, elephants, chimera and snakes. People are gentle and non-obtrusive and sleep upon the porches as goats feed upon the leaves strewn on the road. Tiny shops line the bazaar and are charming in their own way, although one would not know what to do with their goods, were one to buy from them. There is brilliant sunshine after a day of rain, and the sea, never too far away, gives the streets windiness. Music blares from loudspeakers, and noisy buses rumble on the mud path, but they do not jar on one. Everywhere is the presence of the wonderful handiwork of sculptors of long ago, and their descendants continue in much the same spirit. Everywhere the magic of the past inundates and comes upon one very much as the waves of the sea do. It is a constant movement, reassuring one of the continuity of things.

A Silent Encounter

A Silent Encounter

There are two Tamil boys wading in the waves. They are thin and gesticulate to each other as the surf breaks over them, bringing smiles to their faces and dance to their torsos. The movements of their hands is beautiful and intricate, and even from a distance, one realizes that they are deaf mute. They come up on the sand. Their features are very aquiline and they are comely, not in the ordinary sense, but in a painterly sort of way. They come to one still smiling and gesticulating in their expressive and intelligent language. One of them communicates that they have come from the big city, not by airplane, but on a bus, and that they are soon to head back. The other opens a sports magazine and shows off a photograph of his big brother. It seems incredible, but as he points to his mouth and ears and then to his eyes, giving a big smile, he is able to say that he is showing gratitude to God for granting him eyesight. When one thing is taken away, perhaps another becomes intensified in compensation. The manner in which these two boys can see, ordinary humanity cannot do. The joyousness of gratitude in those who possess little or nothing only heightens our own inner poverty. Smiling, the two boys go off, leaving behind an inexplicable aura. At night, one lies on the grass, and one seems to have gone back many years to a kind of childhood where a world lies undisturbed. The moon is coming to fullness among windswept clouds. There are two movements of the clouds, in both directions. Is it the moon that moves? No, it is the clouds. And yet, yes, it is the moon that moves again. The sound of the sea is all engulfing. One has perhaps never communicated so fully with anyone as one did with two deaf mute boys, not even to people one speaks to for hours.

Stones in Time

Stones in Time

One goes for many kilometers along dry, flat countryside, and soon one comes to a hillock that looks commonplace, but conceals Buddhist monuments. It is smaller than one would have expected, for one is at its height in a matter of moments. Walking among the silent and famous ruins, it is easy to see why the site has attracted men for two thousand years since it was built. The strength it emanates is simple and direct. One would come only to look upon the peace that its Buddhas exude, even those that have become headless; they are indeed beyond time. In the modest, austere and small monastery cells, one can imagine the frail bodies of praying monks, encased as they would have been in thick-walled stone. One can almost hear their low breathing in meditation, and feel the human glow in the heart of dull rock.

An Early Home

An Early Home

Far away beyond the hot plains and shrubs, one mounts other hillocks, and comes to human shelters under rocks and in caves that are millions of years old. They protect from the elements and are wonderful to stand within. These are man's oldest homes. Like all residences, they began as shelters, but ended up, even then, in becoming infinitely more. That metamorphosis is something that has not changed for humanity in twenty thousand years. These homes are among the most beautiful in existence; the comforts of water that could be found in a nearby stream, and warmth, that could be created by burning the leaves and twigs from neighbouring trees, seem mundane when compared to the fundamental thrust that the caves present. In seeing the drawings etched on the rock walls, one knows that all the impulses of art are there, that early and that powerful. Yet what the caves represent is much more. It is man in nature, safe from the wilderness, living in beauty and holding life sacred. The preciousness of life is expressed spontaneously and for all time in the simple x-shaped man and animals on the rough stonewalls that could speak meaningfully even to a child.

A Retreat in the Mist

A Retreat in the Mist

Her child is wrapped in the shawl that is tied to her waist and swings as she walks to the town. She carries a long bag of charcoal on her back, and that is to be her earning for the day. She is there on the road that is bordered with pine trees with her sisters, daughters and aunts. Some of them are old and wrinkled, but one can see beauty among them; they come from a faraway village on the slopes each morning to sell their coal. The season is one of rains and mists, of the incessant chirping of crickets in the trees; the brilliant sunsets are unique each evening, and iridescent noons are consistent. The greens of thickly growing trees now assume shades of grey. Silence-inducing clouds that are trapped in the mountains highlight some trees and obliterate others, and they also obscure all but the sounds of insects.

Four boys walk on the road in step with the rhythm of their talk, and it strikes one very deep that they embody innocence in their poverty. By walking behind them for a furlong, one hopes that their simplicity and openness, their uncluttered lives, will rub off somehow on oneself. Perhaps it will come in the manner of a gift that the mountains bestow on one who asks for their blessing. The boys look back at one because they have heard one's footsteps in the mist behind them; then they go about their chatter under the tall pines and beneath the clouds. One's soul is heavy, but lurking not too far away is the ecstasy that glows in sheer innocence. They are poor and dressed in rags, but one's heart leaps out at them, and it is strange in its leaping because it has been burdened with the rub of too much cleverness in other people. Perhaps it is for that reason that it's reaching out to poverty and innocence seems planned and not spontaneous. Perhaps there will come a time when the surrender is unpremeditated, but for the moment, mind holds the sway and thoughts intermingle with the act. And there they are, doing what they do everyday, going home to their villages from their outing in town. They stop at the teashop and buy a little something; perhaps their mother has given them a sack to fill with wheat. They halt a moment and move on, hardly aware of the simplicity of their lives or the beauty of the woods or the silence of time moving on. They are unaware, but they are a part of all this. They are inseparable from the mountain, from the all-obscuring cloud that strayed too low in this season of thick-falling rain and delicate drizzles, and of intoxicated insects.

There is utter abandon in the call of a mountain bird, and this is a thing of everyday, of each moment. The heart is heavy, but ecstasy is not far away; it is there in the eyes of a cow that looks keenly as one passes, it is there in a swift breeze coming up the slope. Animals look at one with stillness and innocence. Ecstasy is there, and the only way to become part of it is not to beckon it, but to see one's own oldness.

A girl leads her three cows to graze on the side of the road and holds a baby lamb in her arms that smells of turds and milk, and is bleating. An old man with marvelous wrinkles and a soiled turban carries a goat strung across his shoulders, and has a time of it, trying to walk with the goat constantly jumping off his back. He asks four men for a pen to write an address, and none of them has one. They say they cannot read or write, and that they only use their thumbs when they have to sign, and don't need a pen. And they smile, puff at their beedis and move on. It is misting; over the hours, little droplets form on the heads of people passing by and on each leaf and pine needle. Everything seemed glazed with water jewels. In houses, roofs drip endlessly and ever so gently. The mist is gauze that has entered everything and remained two days, wrapping the mountain in mystery. It has overtaken everything slowly and vanquished the sun in innumerable dewdrops. There are workers laying fresh tar on the mountain road, and dozens of them are busy clearing the rubble, heating the tar in large canisters, shoveling the gravel onto large trays over wood fires that smoke so heavily, and dripping the melted tar on the road. Then they lay on the tarred gravel and wait for the yellow steamroller to flatten it out between the ropes that border the road where the new tar is being laid. The workers are dark and thin, some are old and others young, and all their women work too. The women wear purple and green saris with silver bands clinging to their waists. By the side of the road, near the plumes of smoke that rise from fires, and protected from the drizzle by torn umbrellas, their babies lie wrapped in rags in small cots, tender under the mist and enshrouded by the clouds. The older children are a little more playful, and while the elders work, they play with them as well. They are a beautiful people, and strange in the environment of the mountains, brought there by the necessity of earning a livelihood. They hand their babies to one happily when one asks for them, and a baby with kohl-smeared eyes scrabbles gently with little hands on one's face.

There is a spider on the windowsill that is about the size of an ant. He has managed to catch one string during his web making between two sticks and is busy going up and down upon it against the breeze as he continues to weave. He can be seen against the dark window frame; against the grass or the mist he would have been invisible. His work goes on for a few minutes and then there is a sudden gust of wind that breaks the fragile thread, and he is left dangling. Undisturbed, he sails quite a long distance around the edge of the window, and will soon start again. Animals and insects are so busy breeding or home making or feeding that it is wonderful just to watch them. It reminds one that only human beings have the capacity to watch, and this is a gift that lies largely unused. The essence of nature persists in the cities as well: an open sky with moving clouds is never too far away, and is our real roof.

It has rained incessantly for three days on this ruin roof. There is goodness in this house that is over a hundred and fifty years old and belonged to a priest who gifted it to the church. Since then, all the visitors who have stayed here were in some way connected to a religious following, and were good people who did charitable works. The musty dining room has a table piled with sweaters for little children that will go to the poor in nearby villages. The church does not have funds to maintain the property, yet it exudes beauty in the way it is. Everything is stained, cracked or peeling and there are innumerable textures on the floors, ceilings, walls, cupboards, tables, chairs, curtains, window grills, fireplaces and chests. The magical patina of time has touched everything. After the rain, there are leaks in many places and pans and buckets have been placed to receive the dribble. Rain sounds softly on the slate tiles of the roof, and in places where there is rusted tin, the rain sounds louder. All the furniture is so old and cracked; in the living room there is a wall of dusty books on religion, and there are recent additions as well. There are so many cracks, stains, scratches, marks and blemishes, yet the rooms are clean, the beds comfortable and one sinks into their soft mattresses under huge quilts, imagining a snowy winter spent reading by the light of the fireside. The living room has an old piano, and three or four visitor's books, full of the names of people who have lived here. The garden is ringed in with blossoming dahlias, the grass is thick and unkempt, and beyond that are the pines that in this season are always grey in the mist. Even in the rain, there are the calls of birds throughout the day; at night there is the sound of thunder and the flashes of lightning. The keeper is a simple man whose face glows with goodness as he brings food on a tray. He must have done good works in his previous life to have the simple life he has in this lifetime, away from the mischief of the world. He has been here since he was twelve years old, and talks of religion as if it were a day-to-day thing, saying that he recognizes those whose hearts are unblemished. There are framed quotations on the walls and quaint watercolours too. In the bedroom a sign says, "God provides resting places as well as working places. Rest then and be thankful when He brings you wearied to a wayside well."

The clouds glide swiftly across the garden, yet for half an hour early in the morning, there has been brilliant sunshine, sliding down the slope that leads to the huts above. Smoke arises from the chimney of each hut, and the slate roof of one hut is aglow with the light of morning. A green bush bursts with scores of pink flowers. Then the mist returns and is white against so many blue mountains. Two fat buffaloes in the garden graze keenly, their horns beautifully curled, and their owner shouts at them and hits them with a branch to move them on. A little dog strays into the garden compound and loiters around an apple tree and then slinks away. The rain comes and goes, sometimes gently and sometimes hard, and changes direction with the wind. The cries of mountain crows in the pines are different to the ones one hears in the plains; they are deeper sounds and do not jar as the harsh cawing one becomes accustomed to in the cities. Other birds twitter, and there is thunder behind the slant of the rain. An urchin whistles past on the road below. The hydrangea in the garden blooms blue, like the clusters one sees everywhere on the hillside. One can almost detect the sound of a rushing river in the wind among the pines, yet it is not so. The house drips in many places after the shower. Parasitic plants on some trees are almost as fully grown as the trees themselves. The moss, ferns, grass and wild flowers that grow wild on roadsides are a delight, and drip and shine endlessly after the rain. A car rumbles by and will splash innumerable puddles that the rain has made on the uneven road. The white sky throws soft shadows afar; the rain starts again, pitter-pattering on the grass. There is more light in the sky than there has been for days. The wind swishes, hurls itself, roars and whispers among unswaying pines, and only frail branches move. The wind brings fragrance of burning wood, and that passes in an instant.

The Swaying Palms

The Swaying Palms

T he coastal city is a delight from the sky, and green as far as the eyes can see. Palm trees cluster the land, leaving just enough room for large tile roof houses under them. Thin roads upon which buses and bicycles move ever so slowly skirt the fields of grey water. An inland sea glitters and on the edge, one can see enormous fishing nets. Once the aircraft has landed, noisy and crowded streets appear in contrast to the ordered quiet one perceived from the air.

The temple is an unimpressive building as one approaches; it is a low-lying single storey pagoda with a sloping tile roof and plaster walls. Two men squat at the entrance, and in the courtyard there are more lungi-clad priests. The circular temple is small and gemlike in its detailing, and lies in the centre of the courtyard with a conical tile roof. One's slippers have already been left at the entrance, but to enter the sanctum sanctorum one needs to doff shirt as well and become as bare-chested as the priests. The wall rises five feet high and is made entirely of rosewood, every inch intricately chiseled with floral and geometric motifs. There are panels carved with Shiva and Ganesha, and lesser deities are smaller in size. The wood is lacquered and glows darkly in strong sunlight, highlighting some features of the wall and giving deep shadows to recesses. Images of the gods are anointed with radiant puffs of vermilion and turmeric. Rows of oil lamps are fixed on iron grids against the backdrop of the wall, each empty and dark from use in rituals. Bells hang low from rafters in the inner temple, covered in the soot from sacrificial flames that are lit underneath. The tiny deity is visible from the doorway and is lit profusely in the pitch darkness that is in contrast to the abundant sunlight outdoors. One cannot take a full circle of the temple because the stone path ends in a small shrine that has images of serpents and gods before it, also powdered in turmeric. In a separate enclosure, a priest sits with a pile of lotus flowers, breaking off each petal and placing it a wicker basket for an offering to the gods. Quietude descends upon one suddenly. The twenty- two priests that live in the temple compound are around somewhere and a few of them walk about doing their chores, yet nothing disturbs the quiet. The flames at the feet of the gods are undying. On auspicious occasions, there are colourful and fierce dances that endure all night, watched by hundreds of people. There are prayers and singing each evening. Outside, the city moves with a slow and noisy pace, but within the walls of the temple is the presence of something else.

It is almost as if temples were built to create a new light in day, an oasis of strange twilight at the height of noon brightness. It softens faces as they moan prayers in inner sanctums, gives an otherworldly glow to eyes and gentleness to fingers as the hands fold in supplication before their god. Then, surrounded in that light, the brightness of oil lamps in an inner temple take on their proper mystical meaning; it is this light that glorifies an all-giving god.

The carvings on the façade have weathered black over hundreds of years. One walks through the large ornate doorway along the passage, marveling at the exquisite sculptures of gods, their dark stone made magical by their size that is larger than life, propped as they are against the backlight of day. The bells, gods, demons, animals and flowers that crowd the pillars partake of ethereal qualities in the dim half-light that is created by the columns blotting out the sky.

The priests are old and thin with heavy markings on their lined foreheads. They are clad in white lungis with the sacred thread slung across their shoulders and down to their waists. They are busy attending to pilgrims in the inner sanctum, passing leaf cups laden with rose petals to the other priests who sit before the deity. They mumble prayers as they perform their ritual, as if not to lose time in doing their good earthly deeds. The gods are always deep within their own shrines, glowing enigmatically in oil lamplight, bedecked in ancient silks and priceless jewels and encased in incense, trapped in garlands and flowers. There are three windows in the inner sanctum and through each, one sees a portion of the sleeping Vishnu: an arm, a torso and finally, a resplendent head, all lit in the golden glow that enhances the deity's mystery. Coins glitter as they land on the metal tray before the god. The priest gives one a ball of sandalwood paste or turmeric to smear on the forehead, a sign that one has sat before one's god in prayer. There are many pilgrims in the spacious courtyard outside, but there is always quietness and unhurriedness with the sound of bare feet walking on smooth granite or the flap of clothing as it brushes past one. Scarcely a breeze enters the precinct because of the high walls. People sit in the pillared hallways and among shadows away from the heat, and they are always with their god.

The brass lamp pole rests on a sculpted tortoise, of which there is one at the entrance of each temple. The discs of the lamps rise in tapering tiers and are lit only for festivals. The entrance is a pillared pagoda of terracotta tiles and all along its walls are thousands of oil lamps. Other lamps hang near the shrine. A brass pillar conceals a sandalwood tree trunk. Sculpted gods stand around a sandy courtyard that has a stone path. The painted wooden façade of the pagoda is intricate in blues, oranges and ochres. The peepul tree before the temple has small stone images at its base where pilgrims have placed a few flowers. Smaller and more anonymous temples at the edge of villages are poorer and simpler in their construction and yet exude another charm. Their scale does not fill one with awe, but they are more modest and perhaps more human, more sincere and conducive to the humility that prayer requires. In being such, they may have captured the spirit of a people with more honesty and directness; one does not always want to be reminded of the greatness of god, one sometimes simply wants to express one's insignificance.

At another temple, there are hundreds of pilgrims, each as dark as ebony, bare-chested and muscular, and dressed in black lungis, their heads sometimes covered in white scarves. There are almost no women among them, as tradition allows only pre-puberty girls or old women to make the pilgrimage. They have come from far and near, keeping their penance for a whole month. Some have found their way to this temple that lies en route to their sacred shrine further away, and rest for a day before venturing to those forested hills. They have wonderful faces that are classic in line on some men, and on others puckish and imp-like, but they seem always to have innocence written across their features. They are open and smile easily, displaying a marvelous curiosity. Their prayers are fervent and they possess only so much as their arms will carry; thus the temple compound is strewn with bundles of clothes. They have found their home, it seems, and are at complete ease in the protection of the temple. They sit and sleep in the courtyards and eat very little. There is a green bathing tank at the bottom of a stairway and some of them wash in it.

There is another shrine outside. In its courtyard there is a tree with hundreds of nails stuck into the trunk. Most are rusted, but some glint anew. Those nails were hammered in by the mentally ill, and it was done with their foreheads serving as hammers. This was the only way in which they could purify themselves and gain their sanity. For all the grotesqueness and the horror of ever-new spikes that jut out among long-rusted nails, the strange tree is very beautiful and strong, like the undying tradition of centuries. How many a madman must have bled from his forehead for the love and protection of a god he had long since become incapable of understanding, and how often he must have returned, miraculously healed. The mind can believe in anything, and the mind that is vulnerable and not whole perhaps does so all the more. The impoverished seeker who had doubtless overcome many hardships to reach here, did, in all likelihood, become sane and healthy through the sureness of his faith, the strength of his determination, the trauma of his penance and his purely physical act of belief. In looking at the leaves of the tree that grow unaffected by the thousands of metal spikes in the body of the trunk, one sees plainly the essence of superstition. Common pilgrims cluster around, but for all their veneration, they can never understand the magical power of the tree. One has to be insane to know its benediction; and the tree is called *amma*.

The entire region seems to be one extended village and engenders a peculiar claustrophobia while traveling between towns because there are no open spaces between the houses and stalls that line the highways. The roads are bad, the traffic unpredictable and noisy. The reason for the unending suburbia is that people found underground water wherever they dug five feet into the soil, and could lay wells easily. The houses were built upon the nodes of transportation rather than in the fields beyond. Earlier, this pattern of thinking led to living along the canals, and today it has meant living by roads where trucks and humble ox carts move. Perhaps the choice of settlements goes deeper than mere convenience; the attraction of crowdedness and being together overshadowed the need for privacy and quiet. When one does chance upon a patch of green paddy in the fields, one breathes free. Suddenly, one sees a chain of mountains in the distance that appear as if cut from paper, trailing off into the horizon. Then again, upon nearing towns, the road becomes crowded and one sees that the delight of open spaces was indeed short-lived.

Sunrise over the town is a beautiful and silent thing. The hills are low in the distance and most of the houses are hidden under palm trees. Landmarks are concealed and it appears as if the sun comes up over lush forest. The mist of early morning creates evaporating layers of grey under the changing scarlet of the sky. The sun seems to come up suddenly, and the earth resumes its familiar colours. There is no breeze and not a bird, and the air is light and cool.

Sunset is deeper, and the forest of palm trees is asleep among the sounds of horning vehicles. The nearby trees are black and their fronds quite still against the sky. Crows fly homeward and are dark silhouettes upon the browning light. Streetlights hide beneath trees and the night becomes hung with bright stars. Insects hover around flowering trees and move in the grass.

A palace is set among the sprawl of villages and is smaller than one's expectation of it. The thing that strikes one immediately is the total absence of colour in the building, and this gives it beauty and dignity. There is only the dark and rich wood that is sometimes superbly carved, and there are bare whitewashed walls. The roofs are of tile that has weathered and darkened and has lost the brightness of terracotta. The only touches of colour in the entire palace are some tiny stained-glass windows, ablaze minutely in orange and blue within the empty halls. The buildings stand at varying heights and appear to be perfectly at right angles to each other. Rooms lead to narrow corridors and to other rooms with steep wooden staircases, and so on to more verandahs and open patios. The innumerable rooms are empty, small and white and the passages have wooden lattice walls through which daylight filters in. The royal women's' room has panels of small drawings framed under glass, and on the highest floor, there are rooms with enchanting frescoes depicting sacred epics. Wooden beams and pillars are ornate, and the doors are heavily chiseled with flower and geometric motifs. Otherwise, there is plain wood, rich and deeply stained so that the grain scarcely shows through. There is a large bed in the royal chamber that is intricately carved from medicinal woods. It is the solitary piece of furniture in the room that one has come to by ascending a narrow staircase. In the long rooms below are rows of grain-storing jars, their black glaze evoking a forbidding austerity. Floors are made of a highly polished material composed of eggshells, charred coconut shells and resin that was pounded flat until it shone. The surface has survived intact for hundreds of years, and even in the dancing hall on ground level that is exposed to the outdoors, it glitters like a dark mirror. The hall is the only part of the palace that is made of stone, and has sculpted granite pillars on all its four sides; in addition, there are potted bushes and trees, lending both shade and colour to the area. There is no grass, but the courtyard is laid out in sand that is a little lighter in colour than the roof. The door of the small temple is shut and an adjacent hall is decorated with wooden statues of dancing and prayerful gods that are brown against the whitewash. Elsewhere, stone gods and demons are displayed upon pedestals, but these were not part of the original décor of the palace, and may even detract from the whole setting. Throughout, the extraordinary austerity and sureness of taste of the people who built the palace greets one, and this is something that the moderns have lost as they went headlong into bright enamel paint and eye-catching design. Even two quaint toilets on the upper floors, made of granite wedged between two passages, evoke simplicity rather than the primitive. Behind the palace, hills rise dry and steep. A road curves down to the village past paddy fields and joins the main thoroughfare in a blare of truck horns amid ox carts. The citadel of kings is swiftly forgotten and its quiet dignity becomes enmeshed in the cacophony of modernity.

A transport boat starts out at the end of a busy street upon hyacinth-clogged waters. A station is piled with rolls of coir mats and a few people sit on the ground. Passengers find places on board and wait, smoking beedis or looking vacantly ahead. It is a rundown boat indeed, with wooden bars obstructing the view.

Soon, a brass bell is rung; it has the sound one hears only in temples, and charms one in spite of being incongruous. The ticket collector flicks pink and green tickets from his tray in exchange for money, and the boat begins to plough through the plants effortlessly.

The journey begins through a narrow water canal. It is a marvel how people living on the banks manage to do so much on such small bits of land; they keep huts with vegetable gardens, have chickens, goats and pigs, and do their washing too. Soon, the town gives way to open paddy fields on both sides of the waterway. Brightly dressed women are bent over paddy crop. Huts by the water's edge are poor and are roofed with thatch, and there are cows and chickens in the courtyards among banana trees. Ponds of tiny white lotus appear and the crows are left behind, replaced by more colourful birds. A woman does her work by the canal. Often, one sees people washing clothes upon cement slabs that jut out into the water. They dash the dripping material on the ground and then spread it out to dry in the sun. A billboard announces the virtues of hair oil and depicts a garishly painted woman who smiles, showing all gums. A group of young men row a boat in unison, and further, a boy washes a calf; both have gentle eyes that peer at one as the boat passes, making giant waves on the calm green water that still has clumps of hyacinth on its surface. Boys swim, dipping in and out of dark shadows.

The fields are immense, green and flat, skirted by mathematically laid-out lines of palm trees; here and there are isolated huts that appear idyllic and quiet and balanced between green land and bright water. Small stations are mere planks on the banks, and the brass bell rings periodically. Egrets fly low and are white, untouched by the surrounding colour of the land. There are impoverished huts and teashops with empty windows, and always the few who want to board the boat. A white pavilion is half hidden behind the trees. Children wave spontaneously and expect no response. Chickens, roosters and goats crowd where there are people, but there are no dogs and no one fishes. Men push canoes against a low wall with slender bamboo, and their vessels rock in the waves they create. The paddy seems to stretch afar on both sides. It is strange to encounter the huts so tiny and alone on the oasis of green and blue, silhouetted against the grey clusters of trees on the horizon.

The boat goes to wide spaces and turns to reveal more trees in the distance ⁺hat garland thin strips of land. A white square appears on the edge of water: a sailboat. Further, four more are seen, their sails made of patches sewn together deftly and their boatmen dark and muscular and often dressed in lungis of fiery colours. Sails puff in a breeze that was not there upon narrow canals, and as the men poke the water with poles, the boats move slowly.

Dragonflies find their way into the boat, glitter in the sun, and soon are gone. A small white bird perches on a stem of floating grass. Apart from these small things, the eyes are entirely taken up with the vastness of the lake-like backwaters, the clear sky and grey horizon that is ringed in with a line of palm trees. A large kitsch church appears; at another station, a solitary red flower blooms and is conspicuous in the blue-grey spaciousness. The toilet on the boat is a delight and consists of a few planks with a square hole open to the gushing water underneath. The water is the same colour as the sky, but a shade darker, and the grey trees accentuate the distinction. The enormous lake is left behind, and the path narrows and fields appear again on the edges. There is another garish temple with a red tractor parked next to it. A man unloads two huge bunches of bananas, sacks of rice, one sack of potatoes and vegetables, one packet of betel leaves, two bundles of beedis, one coil of plastic hose, and one electric motor: his needs for a month. The ticket collector is impatient, but the boat serves as vehicle for village shopkeepers and does this for free. One house is bright with prosperity, but poorer homes reflect more taste and use the traditional materials that are abundant: leaves from the trees for thatch and mud from the land for walls. There is dignity.

There are sheds and boatyards near the town where the boat ends its journey, and one moves through more hyacinths to the jetty. Men bathe on the steps opposite the station; as they push the plants away, they reveal clean water underneath. The boat pulls in and passengers alight noiselessly. Men unload large sacks of grain with agile gestures and few words. A young boy sells bright tickets for a lottery, all printed in a beautiful curly script that has few sharp angles in it and seems more like a picture than a language.

On a winding village road, one comes to higher mountains; one leaves the palm trees of the plains for high trees among rubber plantations. The nearer ranges are green with vegetation and those further away are bare and loom blue in the distance. The road goes downward; velvet hills are clustered with immaculate bushes and there is the familiar fragrance of tea. Small villages are like those in the plains and tiny brooks flow past them. Not far away is a tiny town on the outskirts of a forest. The high trees hide the mountains with their lush foliage, and nearby is a wildlife sanctuary. There are monkeys and the sound of marvelous birds in the air that resounds with their echoes.

A lake was created when the river that meanders through rolling hills was dammed. Everything seems charmed with a cleanness that only nature knows. The land slopes gently to the water and is thickly overgrown with plants. One is told not to make a sound, as this would alert the animals, yet the sputtering old motorboat is itself the only noisy presence in the sanctuary. One chances upon a family of elephants on their morning stroll, and they have a dignity they cannot know in their bonded state in the towns. Black stumps stand in the lake. When water flowed into the valley, all but the tallest trees were submerged. An occasional bright bird perches on a stump, but otherwise, an absence of life in the area strikes one. The magnificent hills, the water and the sky are silent and empty. The forest sleeps in the day and lives only after dark. Dew is heaviest on the grass in the early morning, and with it the quietness of the day returns to the forest. The grasses lead to humid and leaf-laden ground, and the sun coming into the elfin light under the trees mingles with the fragrance of new shoots. A flying squirrel floats from branch to branch, its resplendent tail accentuating its grace. Crickets have stopped chirping and egrets in the fields are silent in flight. They perch on barren tree trunks and turn instantly brown; when they lift upward into the air they are white again. A rustle in the trees reveals monkeys jumping in and out of sunshine. The forest trees give way to more grasslands and the blue flash of the lake appears again. A breeze cools as one treads dry grasses and twigs; even in destruction there is cleanliness and thrift in the jungle. Another group of elephants roams like so many slowly moving boulders and the strangeness of man in nature overtakes one; for a moment, one feels how alien the jungle has really become to humanity.

The small town is lined with cluttered shops on both sides; the teashops are the only empty ones, with chairs and tables in them. The vegetable shops are multicoloured and terracotta stalls are monochrome. There are grocers and provision stores and box-like paan and cigarette stands. Spice-selling establishments look more like offices than shops and they are dealers in cardamom, their rooms full of women sifting the light green pods in straw trays and filling sacks with them. The bus station is noisy from there, enormous monster buses rumble through the narrow and bumpy streets to larger towns. Garish hotels, a mosque and a temple are tucked away also between shops; the town is one storey high. In the afternoons it is empty but fills with strollers in the evenings when shops become weakly lit with naked electric bulbs. One sees kerosene lanterns that can now be found only in the smaller places. Villages around the town are humble, set among green fields with the rolling hills behind them. Groups of no more than six or seven huts are encircled by bushes. Women carry bundles of twigs on their heads, and in the evening, the cows are still grazing. The needs of the villagers are few, but when even those cannot be met with, there is hunger and want. It is quiet and away from the bigger roads; blue smoke rises from chimneys near the dirt paths, and homes become surrounded in a hazy nimbus from wood fires that hangs idly in the air. Boys ride bicycles joyfully on the paths and passing villagers always find a word to exchange with each other. The green inundates one, and as the sun sets and the stars begin to shine, tiny oil lamps are lit against mud walls upon broken benches in front of doorways and in windows. The sound of crickets becomes apparent, and another day is done.

A village fair occupies both sides of the road and the sandy field behind. Everything imaginable for a home is available; housewives are happy with armfuls of things for their kitchens. The shops are bright with steel utensils, and brown with terracotta pots. The straw mat shops are beige and the food stalls radiate colour. People squat on palm leaves that occupy the whole field. Men sell fluorescent candy that vies with the plastic shops in hue to big-eyed children, yet the toy-sellers are the brightest stalls on the sand, their wares strung across a single pole. Everything is for under a rupee: goggles, dolls, whistles, balls, playing cards, cars, horns and balloons.

There are quaint tile roof houses on the waterfront of the city, and tugboats behind large modern ships on the water. A palace has extraordinary murals depicting the Ramayana and the Puranas, in which ornately costumed gods sit among frail lotuses, burnished orange by time. These seventeenth-century masterpieces lie largely undiscovered, and scarcely talked-about. On the shore, the fishing nets are spectacular, like a row of giant spiders with their webs contained entirely under their legs. Fishermen gossip in the afternoon and some men lower a net into the water, but bring up nothing. There is a church among elegant bungalows and contains a famous and humble grave. There is a coir factory on a small island where workers weave mats in sheds. Rough brown rope litters the floors, and the tuft is strewn everywhere in glowing puffs of colour. The material is beaten and fluffed in half-light and this creates an unreal atmosphere. On another small island, a rundown palace serves as a hotel. The big boats plying the shore disturb a contemplation of nature in an otherwise picturesque setting. There are many fragrances in the tiny bazaar of the old town. Behind shops in the sunny courtyards, ginger is dipped in lime and blue powder to dry, and the black pepper that is spread out on mats has pigeons pecking at it. Betel nuts are piled against old walls. Workers lift huge sacks of spices and hoist them onto trucks that can scarcely negotiate the narrow alleys. There are dungeon-like antique shops in the market where dust adds to the cost of their goods. At their doors, men stitch gunnysacks to pack their products. A fabled synagogue is there among the shops and has blue and white Chinese tiles on its floors, each unique in design. Chandeliers hang on chains from a gaudy ceiling, and the keeper, one of a small and dwindling community, opens a cupboard quietly and shows visitors the silver and gold crowns it contains. The teashops outdoors are dark and abandoned, and there are cobblers and torch-repairers on the street who sit idle. The activity in the marketplace is brisk, and elsewhere, the pace is so slow as to be negligible.

An Untouched Atoll

An Untouched Atoll

The ship sails slowly out of harbour, leaving the small vessels that have seagulls hovering over them behind, leaving the boy in the canoe for which the waves are too big as he bails the water out with a tin can. The sun sets over large nets and one leaves the tongue of beach behind too. There are orange flecks on the water and a clear horizon; one almost eats the breeze.

The stars are big and seem to sway over the deck, and the dawn is slow in coming. When the sun rises, it does so suddenly over a cloud that has grown out of the greying sea, and drops pink radiance on its outlines. One immediately senses the cleanness of nature and remembers the complications of man, two things that seem always in a precarious balance in each human life.

One leaves the ship upon nearing the island, and a tiny boat goes ashore since it alone can negotiate shallow coral reefs. Alongside the main island are other smaller ones that may as well belong to cartoon strips: just a few palm trees on dots of land in the sea. The morning light plays along the waves and as one goes over the reefs, the water becomes clear. In the pristine morning, nature's benediction shines abundantly upon all. There is quietness in nature, but noise where men are, and one lives poised between the two.

Over calm water, the boat sputters to the jetty, having passed thick vegetation and a red and white lighthouse. There are few permanent structures among the thatch roof huts. The scores of bicycles and the solitary van parked in front of a building mar the simplicity of the setting. A tarred path under shady trees becomes a sandy track and passes huts in the woods. Soon one is at the tip of the island. The water is a magnificent turquoise green near the coral beach. Waves break far away in a fine white line and beyond that is deep blue water. Here, as if enchanted, it glints a transparent green. The open sea is at a distance and its waves break and curl over rocks; here on the beach, seaweed stretches under the waves for an instant and disappears into pure foam.

People are dark and beautiful with wonderful smiles and an open curiosity. The men wear lungis and the women long dresses and have large rings set in rows upon their earlobes. Children are charming and so like the adults, only more spontaneous in their warmth. Among the thatch roof huts, there are a few brick cottages. There is a teashop ion the pathway, with tiny windows cut through its bamboo and rattan, revealing a bare interior, devoid of customers.

The evening sun sets between two islands that are studded with palm trees. It is a time when the whole earth seems to become a moving water world. Everything is set in motion: the sea, the sky and the changing light. Only the silhouetted islands are immobile and strongly rooted. There are small black flecks in the distance; they are fishermen walking knee-deep in the reef. A rowboat glides by as if to seal a picture. There is infinite peace in the sky, in the clouds that engulf the dipping sun and in the shimmering silver of the water. The sky glows for a long time after the sun has gone, as if reluctant to be vanquished by a tender crescent moon. It happens so patiently that one does not notice that a complete transformation has occurred before one. It is as if day and night were of one material, and one was hanging lost between the two, unknowing of the soul of nature.

The sands are white because they are eroded coral, and they have the texture of talcum powder. The water is a startling emerald. When the waves come in, the sand on the bed flows free, and it is like swimming in milk.

From a height, one sees only palm trees covering every inch of land, leaving a white rim of sand at the edges. Beyond, there is just sea. There is a silence, and within that, the sound of the sea exists. On another part of the island, there is calm water because the waves break far away where the reefs end. A tiny offshoot island is skirted in white sand, quiet upon the blues and greens of water. It has a tiny lagoon that seems even more serene, if that were possible, half concealed in trees and undisturbed by anyone. Not a bird is in the air, not a hut can be seen on the ground.

The coral on beaches has turned grey with age and has been rounded by the movements of water. The clarity of the water comes again upon one. There are beaches where never a footprint was made, and their sands have flattened hard and clean. There are black palm tree stumps upon some beaches, charred and upturned, revealing bits of coral caught in the roots, and sometimes, bits of blue nylon string from the nets of bygone fishermen.

The sea is calm and glassy, and from the deck one can see fish that have neared the surface. One chances upon a little from the bounty of the deep and even that seems plentiful. Flying fish flee the water in unison, blue in body and brown–winged, like miniature jets at an air display. They fan out in perfection for hundreds of yards over rippled water and then are gone forever. A shark swirls menacingly a few feet underwater and then is lost in the gloom. A buoyant school of dolphins leaps in and out of dark ripples. The movements of nature convince one that perhaps when living beings are at their highest, they are at play.

The sun sets in the same way that it arose, among open spaces, pouring itself into the sea by stretching its perfect circle into an oval, and emptying its rim of red into a vibrating glow of greys. There is peace in the heart at seeing this periodically; it is something bound in time that hints at the presence of a deeper source. The sinking sun could have been touched if one had spread out one's fingers. The beach could have stirred with its first footprints, one had but to take a step. It was not to be. They had both been too close, and were best left as they were, the one a thing of every day, the other so rare to find.

The Living Ruins

The Living Ruins

The river is slow in the dry season, and at the edge of leaf-covered mounds, is so still that it reflects the trees perfectly. There are rocks in the water and then it turns to rapids. It continues gently to lower areas, curving around verdant land. The water-carved rocks are smooth and warm in the sun, the water cool and refreshing.

Women lead cows through an archway in the fortress. They are going home to their village within the walls. Indifferently built houses line the narrow streets among the shops. Tiny temples sparkle with fresh whitewash on each street, and there are garland makers in the compounds before them with flaming yellow baskets of flowers. The women buy them to decorate their doorways. Children hover around one, curious at new passers-by. The walls of the fort are of solid granite, their blocks piled geometrically. Through other gateways, one glimpses at the river that is omnipresent in the land as it flows flat past paddy fields.

A road climbs past many small settlements to a hill temple. It is white and large and without much character, but the panorama of small town and villages from there is splendid, as they lie among the hillocks at sunset. Every shade of green is there, turning grey and blue. A magnificent mausoleum is white, and further, minarets fade into the distance. Clumps of tile-roof villages appear among paddy that shines where the water in the fields is full. Squirrels run up the walls of the hill temple, but there are no birds. In the village below, old men sit under enormous trees and in the fields, women work on the rice crop.

Evening is a quiet time by the river. The water is mirror-smooth and echoes the browns of the sky between the foliage. A fragrance of flowers ignites the air among the sounds of a million crickets. A necklace of wild ducks floats up above and frogs leap on wet ground. One crushes leaves underfoot under very old trees that send their branches low over the ground. Palm trees curve whimsically against the bare sky. One hears evening birds. A semi-circular haystack lies behind a small white tomb that has a dark and weathered dome. The hills in the distance remain grey as the sky changes colour.

The slowness of the river in this season strikes one again, yet one can hear it ruffling over rocks even before one comes to it. The path among fields curves, and the sun is all gold. There are small birds around the tomb and crows in the sky. The river is flat and silent until it reaches the rocks. All the colours of the setting sun come to it through the lattice of trees on the rich land of the other shore. Insects hum in the evening light, finer than the sounds of the water that is larger and more whole. The verdure of the fields comes even to the water edge, where bunches of leaves grow between rocks. The river becomes a grey gold silk. A tree hangs over the water, dropping insects that create fine ripples that evaporate quickly into the liquid. Here, the water suddenly hits rocks and creates countless textures before moving on. The water is always new, and perhaps a white egret that floats over it can feel its freshness. A row of ducks flies past while the smaller birds are freer in their movements as they fly up and down making their own patterns.

The grasses are dry, but further, they turn green against the tree, outlined against the stillness of the water and the curls of delicate ripples. Rocks lie like amphibians that have forgotten how to move; there are many placed close to each other; their shapes are diverse and invite the imagination to create familiar creatures from their forms.

A dragonfly zigzags, and small birds fly high, their black dot shapes becoming smaller and wavering until they are swallowed by the sky against the white blaze of cloud that slowly changes form. The crisscross of ripples is a shadowlike pattern against the shore grass. Leaves upon a tree are shiny and new and ever so still against the moving water. The land is silent and green. The whites of the ruffling water are a reflection of clouds. The shine upon the water is white too. A mirror world is juxtaposed against a dull terrain, harsh forms vie with those that are polished; the sky is hollow upon an earth that is full and bustling down to its minutest details, to the last insect that whirrs before being lost in the subtle light. The grasses, burned leaves and charred ground are still even in the murmuring breeze. A leaf floats by on the water, gains the rapids and becomes anonymous. It is easy to forget the presence of the sky, but it is ever changing; now, a cloud becomes a streak of grey that alternates with white. Birds seem to weave between two bands; three fly past in unison as if their wings were turned to the same force, and they are soon followed by a string of fluttering ducks whose formation changes spontaneously, as if it were let loose in the heavens by a sudden gust of wind. Another leaf drops from the tree and creates a stir before balancing upon silken water and being wafted in the current to the foamy rocks. Is one's heart free with the everyday joyousness and inexplicable beauty of nature? An insect flits to and fro upon the wet surface, making many patterns and stitching its movements with needles of light. A fish leaps over the insect and then both are gone. How suddenly the silken water becomes turbulent as its pool-like stillness succumbs to a great motion. There are silent puddles in the body of the rock that glow with skylight, like emptiness entrapped in darkness. One's heart is at play with the soul of nature. Two large black birds glide in the sky and are lost in the cluster of leaves that is silhouetted against the white sky of evening. Tiny insects make an invisible mesh in the air and disperse into nothingness. The palm trees are tall and still as if spellbound by the hour. Now suddenly, many insects appear upon the river and make myriad patterns. Small fish leap and a butterfly flits to the water's edge past dry leaves and rocks that jut over the surface. The sun has turned to blood, hidden behind the dark of the trees, and the water imitates it with a pink band upon its grey body. The forms of foliage shimmer darkly upon the pulsating pink that begins to spread like liquid. Observing the movements of the elements reminds one that one cannot fight the flow, even while one sees insects that are trying to go against the tide, or like the fish that leaps backwards wants to do. They ultimately become lost among those rocks; the ripples are in the end dissolved into a larger force. Trees brood against a sky that darkens, and will become thicker as the season changes; the river will become higher, and the rocks will submerge in the strong current. But perhaps at this time of change and in this altering light, the scene hints at the existence of many worlds and mixed moods, all caught in the same place for one memorable moment. In seeing this, one is at peace. One is like the leaf that fell and drifted upon the river and disappeared. In one's going, has there been peace? In the flutter of the dark butterfly upon the glow, has there been an awareness of something quite beyond the scene that is immediately before one? Is one conscious of that which one comes upon so easily and yet passes over, unnoticing?

By the side of the road near the fields, there is the tiniest temple that looks to be two or three hundred years old. It is just a place where the villagers come to pray and leave jasmine blossoms on the small Ganesh image that is hidden from the breeze. Village women carry baskets on their heads, followed by their children as they walk past. The breeze makes the sugar cane stalks quiver. One passes the fields, going along the dirt track. There are mango groves, and one comes to the river where there is another temple. There are rocks in the river and a woman washes clothes as monkeys leap among the trees. Dogs sleep in the courtyards of tiny buildings, some of which are in ruins and have ivy growing over them. The compound of the main shrine is whitewashed and has a black deity at its centre that is decorated with golden flowers. A priest passes, carrying offerings, and disappears around a corner. Leaves festoon painted doorways in the inner shrine, below which the river flows over rocks. There are white birds against the water, and there is quietness in the afternoon. A breeze is there too, and grey shadows shake on the white pavilion walls. More priests are at their chores, hoisting buckets of water up to the sanctums from the river. Everywhere, the deities are black and shine with oil against the matte whitewash. Old trees in the courtyards lead to the water where men wash on the steps. A pair of squirrels plays among the sculpted towers, and underneath, images of Ganesh and Hanuman, and a black and vermilion lingam seem to be at eternal rest. People have laid out their wet clothes on the wide stone platforms, and children swing from swooping branches. In another place, a tree has broken through a wall and virtually overtaken a temple compound. Little children bring guavas, and the priests of the tiny shrine give prasad of halva and bananas wrapped in leaves to outstretched little palms.

There are gilded wooden palaces of exquisite intricacy laid out on acres of lush lawn, and these are visited by hundreds of people every day. Yet it may be the anonymous and obscure village temples, hidden among the fields and often by the river, that speak through their silence of a humble and unswerving daily devotion, a love of god and a gratitude for the simple existence bestowed upon them.

Another temple upon a hill is a modern-day structure and without much character. Walking down the hill on old granite steps, one comes upon an enormous black Nandi carved from a single rock, sitting impressively underneath trees where monkeys play. The image is garlanded and adorned with turmeric and flowers. The small door that has been cut into the rock behind the Nandi is an entrance to the cave where the kindly pundit lives. To a side, another rock has been embellished with cow dung pats that make a charming and naïf pattern.

The temple is raised on a square platform and is a granite jewel that is small, flat and perfect. The entrance pillars are of stone and have been turned on a lathe. There are three towers on the site, and the entire temple is patterned upon a star-shaped floor. Every inch is richly carved with figures of gods and people, animals and flowers. One moves slowly around the building in order to absorb each detail; there is so much to take in that it is impossible to retain everything in the memory. Below, on the level of the stone floor, are small sculptures of elephants and gods. The courtyard is ringed in with a low wall; sixty-four cells stand behind the pillared hallways. The inner sanctum of the temple is unlit. Three cells contain images of a black Vishnu that is scarcely revealed in the light that filters in through a small door. The stone is carved with so much complexity that it resembles lace. The god stands poised with various instruments in his many arms and is bedecked in jewels that reach his knees; he has splendid headgear, and has stood thus for eight hundred years. Outside, each facet of the temple is intricately and richly carved. Below the panels of the gods, there are lines of birds, elephants, dancers, flowers, horses and more elephants. Above are canopies and doorways, and these carvings proceed on to tapering towers that consist of panels of flowers, ornaments and figures of gods, until one is under the sky at the top of the temple, that does not reach too high. Here are warriors on horses and yogis in meditation and tiny divine figures in various poses. Above this are lovers, carved a few inches high. Each of the three towers contains a Vishnu deep in their heart, hidden from daylight and in utter darkness, like a secret thrice contained. A yogi sits on the outer wall with a fire that rages all round him. Demons and chimeras are encircled in bowers between the turrets of miniature temples carved into the stone. A god dances upon a five-headed snake. A divine being stands beneath a flowering bush while another sits in meditation with two conches in his hands. A pair of men on an elephant follow others on horses that push a chariot carrying a twosome that comes behind a soldier with a shield. There are a couple of camels with soldiers under them in front of three horses. There are more army men, and twin elephants with riders. Tiny lovers are ensnared in blossoms, and underneath them, the gods stand on the brink of their samadhi, supported by a band of musicians among rows of fine floral circles, with horses, warriors, and elephants, all in procession. Hunters chase deer, and men stand around a tree. A goddess dances, entrapped in garlands and wonderful jewels underneath a flowering bush, and is surrounded by her drummers and tambourine players. She is in rapture and retains a serene expression. Another goddess stands upon a bull and presses down a dwarf. A footman is devoured by a demon. Images of the gods are only two feet high and are at eye level, so that they could be executed in great detail and remain in full view. There are rows of swans below the gods that have magnificent tails. Chimeras swallow flowers and are followed by musicians with their hands raised in unison. There are blossoms and more militia on horseback, and the procession of elephants reaches to the floor. A god poses with weapons in his hands. He has a lotus and fruit and is protected by a tree. There are yet more carvings above him. Elephants crush soldiers and horses leap over footmen. Warriors armed with taut bows in their hands are pulled by horses while swords are raised behind them. A goddess sits upon a lotus in meditation, perfectly calm in her gaze. A god sits with his consort on knee upon a throne, their feet resting upon lotus. A god dances with his garlands and jewels flying to a side and his head tilted. Behind him, a wreath is mounted with a monster. Another god plays music and dances simultaneously. A god kneels under a tree, hoisting a lesser god with consort ion his arms. A king rides a bejeweled elephant and carries a woman with him. A monster sits with a goddess upon his knee. The gods stand with corn in one hand and weapon in another and are in contemplation. A four-headed Brahma is there with his instruments and sandalwood rosary in hand. Krishna plays the flute and Ganesh dances. Women sit under parasols with babes in arms. Lovers are caught in different poses, in couples and in groups.

The innumerable carvings have depicted the fullness of the universe and yet remain essentially a rendition of an inner reality; the within and the without are in harmony and have been given life in stone for all time. Mallitamma and his many sculptors have given a pellucid drop of purity to the world and it rests among unknown fields and hamlets in perennial silence.

The clouds and breeze constantly change the light, and the land becomes barren as one moves along. The rocky hillock has a temple at its summit that can be seen from afar. One reaches the tiny village and comes past ruins. Plants grow through the rocks of the uneven steps, and two platforms lead to a large tank of shimmering grey green water. A pillared hallway surrounds it on four sides and there are small temple towers behind. It is unused but unusual in its beauty. Only the local villagers seem to come here sporadically; the neglect the ruins have suffered perhaps also gave it a chance to evolve away from jealous eyes into a place of rare character and austere quietude. Over rough pathways, one comes to a skeletal monument that is only brick and mortar, its upper layers of stonework and plaster having eroded. The roofs have grass growing on them, but there is as yet a magnificent circular pavilion with detailed reliefs upon its domes; flowers and resplendent figures are sheltered under a central tower. The pillars with tiny drawings of the gods rise upward to figures at the very top. A few pilgrims bathe in the tank or sit by its steps, but it is an unvisited place. It is undiscovered and therefore unspoiled, and perhaps has had the last word in its battle with time and man's intrusions. In being able to remain untouched, it has succeeded in remaining as a ruin should remain. It belongs blissfully to the chameleons, pigeons and squirrels that have made it their abode. People sit in the village below the hillock on the mud and sell vegetables.

A bullock cart brings in more sacks of grain, and schoolchildren appear from nowhere and run about in bright uniforms on their way home. A painted temple on the hill path is still used and leads to a doorway where one can leave one's shoes. There are small flat-roofed pavilions all along the way upward, upon granite steps that have become disjointed over the years. A silence and aloneness overtakes one among the old trees, and seems to be the emotion that would come to one unasked, as if it were the place itself that engendered it so effortlessly within one. A rock has a faded apsara painted upon it, and one passes her, going through a second archway upon the steps that take a turn upon the hill. More pavilions punctuate one's ascent. There are charred stones under some archways, the vestiges of fires burned by the pundits of the temple. There are monkeys, and a priest runs down the steps, carrying an empty brass pot. Another is on his way up, and pauses for a moment while balancing a pot of water on his head. He mounts the steps slowly and chants mantras as he goes. The tile-roof village is left quite far below, among flowering Jacaranda and Bougainvillea; beyond those trees the land is dry under the grey sky. Monkeys play above a small temple that has a figure of Hanuman carved upon it. The image is strangely appropriate, and seems to freeze the movements of the god's creatures in stone. Trees are dappled with lichen, as is the enormous rock behind them, and the area is not free from the graffiti that even unfrequented ruins are prone to collect. A small Ganesh and minor deities have been chiseled into the rock. The final step leads to the door of the temple at the summit. It has weathered pale with exposure to the elements, and the patina of its stone facades, five-tiered tower and enormous copper door lend it simple charm. A brass panel shields the sanctum and depicts Vishnu's ten avatars. Inside, people are at prayer. The priest passes a flame around, and pilgrims wave their palms over it and bring their fingers over their eyes. The roof of the temple is uneven and one views the dry countryside as sounds of singing schoolchildren come up from the village where one can now see a pond. There are small clusters of trees and hillocks protrude from the flat landscape and fade into the haze among intermittent terracotta villages.

The bus gets very full by the time it reaches the village; at least a hundred and fifty passengers alight from it. The return journey is comparatively empty, and the bus goes over mud roads through barren country, stopping wherever one or two people hail it. Usually, the villagers see the bus from far away and run over the fields in order to catch it, and more often than not, the vehicle screeches to a last-minute halt. At one such stop, a man hauls three or four gigantic basketfuls of flowers wrapped in cloth. The driver has to move to a side so that the baskets can be pushed in from the front of the bus, since that is the only way they can be accommodated, and he does this without any complaint. The flower seller sits down beside his bobbing belongings as the bus rumbles forward. One wonders, where did he possibly find all those flowers in this barren land? From how far away these flowers come and with how much patience they are sewn into blazing garlands, all to be sold for a pittance in the streets of the city. The driver takes one wreath and places it carefully between two windows at the front of the bus. No matter how rickety and poor the buses are, there will always be fresh flowers near the driver's seat and a place for everyone to get on, despite numbers. The land is rocky, and the road is still under construction; when it nears a village does it become metalloid, only to turn to mud again further on. A lake lies somewhere on the slightly undulating terrain, but one sees only rock and shrub or the occasional hillock in the distance as one moves. Bright little schoolchildren get on the bus and dawdle about, chattering among themselves. Some are barefoot, but others wear shoes, depending on what their parents can afford for them. Their uniforms are either pink or blue, and always crisp and fresh. The bus halts again at a village. There are cows and people sit about on the street, some drinking from coconuts that seem to be the only things to buy, for there are not the bottled soda drinks of bigger villages here. Children that are at play; throughout the lifetime of wild animals, there is total play, and human beings seem to forget this as they grow. In the village, only the children are playing, without any burden or anguish. They are at ease everywhere and are mainly within their own world; perhaps that is the secret of their innocence. There are spontaneous smiles on faces, even on adults, and there is happiness. It convinces one that it is simplicity that the villagers live within, and not poverty. They make do with very little and are fascinated by the things that come from the big world that is so alien to them. Their curiosity does not contain possessiveness or craving, and in that too they are childlike and unspoiled by the rush that modernity brings in its wake.

The palace in the city is an enormous edifice and extraordinarily gaudy in form, colour and in the materials it has used in its building. There is painted plaster, marble of all textures, stained glass, gilded woodwork, crystal, mirror, velvet and satin, silver doors and brass and much else besides among the hallways of ornamental pillars and roomfuls of paintings. It is an overload, but the villager who lives with bare essentials in his terracotta hut finds all this overwhelming and awe-inspiring; his short visit is wonderstruck and becomes in itself a thing to marvel at. The gardens outside the city continue the fascination, and are electrically lit at night in all colours among gushing fountains that nevertheless echo the ebullience of simple village folk.

Villagers play drums on the street before the hillock of the single brown granite. Seven hundred steps have been carved into the rock and lead to the enormous statue of Bahubali at its broad apex. There are a few Jain pilgrims dressed in white climbing up for a darshan of the ancient prince-saint. From the top, the view of the surrounding countryside arrests the footsteps as one looks out to the stony hillocks in the distance among fields, past the tank of green water near the temple below. There are terracotta roofs amid palm tree plantations and paddy crop. The ascent on the hill has been on sheer rock; among the small shrines and huge boulders that are perched on the ground there is a doorway adorned with two stone elephants and the image of a goddess. One enters, and the first thing one notices are the feet of the statue. Only that much is first visible; they are considered to be the most sacred part of his figure and are gigantic. A climbing creeper has been carved on his legs because the saint's penance lasted a millennium and plants grew over his motionless body that was in deep meditation. As one nears, one sees that the grey stone figure is two storeys high. It is curiously disproportionate and naïf in its sculptural appeal. It brims, nevertheless, with the fullness of an inner balance rather than a physiologically correct interpretation of the human body. The icon's inherent serenity and dignity are thereby all that more persuasive, even to the unlettered pilgrim who comes in prayer. There is a narrow and covered amphitheatre in front of the image, and on a small platform, priests chant standing at his feet, carrying a flame on a silver tray. The offering of flowers and sandalwood has been made and its fragrance wafts to where the visitors sit. Bells are rung. Prayers are unending and can be heard at all hours of day and night. They are as everlasting as the fragile jasmine garlands that entwine his toes, for the blossoms are frequently replaced with fresh ones by the priests as more and more pilgrims offer them. Once every twelve years, thousands of Jain pilgrims gather for a ceremonial anointing of the figure with sacred water, ghee, milk, turmeric paste, coconut water, honey and vermilion powder. They watch the festivities in complete silence, and depart without having uttered a word. Yet the sanctity of the site is apparent even ordinarily when only a few people are present, as ritual prayers continue to be carried out every day without fail.

The entrance of the temple at Belur has the usual tower; behind it the main shrine is flat roofed and squat, in different shades of granite. The many small carvings and minor shrines all rest on a star-shaped ground plan. It is a wonderful monument, yet it is the later temple at Halebid, further into the countryside, where the sculptural style blossomed to unique perfection. The heightening of aesthetic sensibility soars with an unparalleled intensity of vision; the elaborate carvings have turned stern rock to delicate ocean spray with the wand-touch of the chisel. The temple may well be the most intricately executed monument in existence, yet it is superbly controlled in its ornate labour. It is just right, and in a taste that transcends the barrier of time. It possesses a quality that is perhaps unsurpassed anywhere, yet remains mysterious and inexplicable to the viewer. The exuberance that it was witness to a thousand years ago became total because of its link to fine thinking, a generous patronage, a vast literature and deep religion. The plea of the temple is to the highest faculties of man; it expresses the finest mental experience that human beings have known, and this is accomplished with sincerity and unswerving sureness. An incalculably complex structure reveals a cosmic vision of staggering depth that does not exclude the quotidian from within its fold. This is because doing and being formed a unity; mysticism portrayed what was rare, yet made it appear of access to the ordinary. Innumerable hands created as if they belonged to one mind. They worked with an exalted consciousness for eighty years as if it were that of one transcending moment. Yet all its minute flawlessness looks from afar as no more than a mere grey rectangle of stone; only upon nearing does the temple display each lavishly executed centimetre to even the most undiscerning eye. The soapstone turned out to be a most appropriate vehicle for the temple's creation: its softness allowed for great detail in implementation, yet with yearly exposure to the elements, it hardened to become impermeable. Countless artists of known stature worked anonymously with sharpened awareness and a lifelong dedication. Their inspiration did not waver; in fact, for them the physical became the cosmic. The marvelous figures from sacred texts are not so much what man has invented, but rather, beings that embody the experience of the human mind. They express the pinnacle to which it can soar and the divinity that it makes known and therefore possesses as part of its intrinsic nature. Yet there is room enough in that vastness even for insignificant human detail: a monkey tugs at a woman's sari on a panel; elsewhere a dancer twists her toes and there are wrinkles underfoot; another dancer unloosens a bangle on her wrist by the gravity and swing of her arm. Faces are serene and perfect, yet no two are alike; the number of figures bewilders the worshipper, reminding him of human limitation. Yet the carvings of intermingling earthly and divine beings are only half life-size, intuitively keeping human scale in mind. The gods can be touched if one were to stretch out one's hands, and yet one would reach only their feet, as if only obeisance to them were permissible. In the pilgrim's brief visit there is experience enough for many years of refection and wonder at what is the toil of human beings in praise of their maker and an essentially humble offering.

It seems to be an obscure village in the middle of nowhere, yet people come to it in large numbers because of its shrine. It is garishly painted, but it was here that a saint took an oath to look after the distress of pilgrims for seven hundred years after his death. The people have a simple faith that has endured the centuries in between. They bathe in the river where the rocks are and eat in a small canteen before going home. There is a whitewashed shrine on the rocks with a small Nandi at its base, where people put flowers. It is more beautiful than the bright temple, but is of no importance. The people come to it after a bath in the river, walking barefoot over hot rocks. An old man sings in the dusty street. There are chickens in the verandah of a hut and a naked child swings on a cot. Buses raise dust and people walk in the sunlight against that haze. The land is dry. One can see hillocks that are spiky with boulders, but little else. It is very hot in the day, but the stars at night are large and bright.

Moving on, the landscape becomes stonier and eventually semi-desert. There are more hillocks and many boulders along the way, and some paddy fields that strike one because of their incongruity. The tilled mud rises to the boulders, and even the clearly delineated clouds that float past have the appearance of rock. Sunflower fields are ablaze, and a boulder among them has been whitewashed with a door carved into it, turning it into a temple. It is difficult indeed to imagine how the people of the region work on the roads and make them, with much hard labour that is so poorly rewarded. When roads are rough and broken, as they are here, one must remember that they were made for bullock carts and not modern cars, and it is a privilege to be on them at all. Each stone was broken and laid with bare hands, the tar heated and poured, the wood for burning brought in the same way under the heat and dust of the arid plain, very far from shade and water. It may be a labour that can earn the worker a place in heaven; and going through the unspoiled countryside of exquisite beauty, one is certain that it does. The black and red soil enriches the land generously, past tiny villages where there are sometimes local fairs, past dry plains and naked hillocks.

The temple within the ruin city is still used and lies behind a small bazaar. A baby elephant keeps the pundit company among the stones of that have worn away to an orange-black, overlooking the whitewashed towers of the courtyard. There are monkeys, squirrels and many birds, and a three-headed icon of Nandi near the door symbolizes universal consciousness. One is asked to clasp a wishing stone and told that the fingers will move to join at its base automatically to make one's dream come true. In the inner sanctum of the Shiva temple, beside the natural lingam, the pundit breaks coconuts and returns them to pilgrims with bananas and flowers. Outside is a shrine to the daughter of Brahma.

The ruins spread above and behind the temple among startling boulders. There are monuments all round as one takes the steps upward to a passageway between rocks, and comes to a Ganesh image. It is enormous and fits between pillars, locked behind wire-mesh doors. A deserted pavilion holds a smaller god called the mustard seed Ganesh, and neither image is worshipped because they are both broken. Placed among sugar cane fields and a trickling stream is a magnificent Narasimha, his giant form projecting ultimate strength through perfect symmetry. His fierce lion form is calm, and his balance profoundly cosmic under the hooded serpent. He was made from the materials of the area, just another boulder. Nearby, a massive lingam rests in a pavilion over a pool of water and seems strangely modern in its minimal lines. Horses and chimera guard a temple elsewhere, among square doors and ornate pillars, and a courtyard that is overgrown with grass. Hallways and cloisters encircle the monument. The force of sculptures and temples is such that even boulders in the landscape take on the presence of more pavilions and shrines, and glow enigmatically with the gold of sunset. There is a magnificent temple dedicated to Krishna, with pavilions in the courtyard. Below it, the river flows over many rocks. There is a pergola to its side that was the home of a famous musician. The main temple is a rare delight, but its hallways are sadly crumbling, as are its gates and stone chariot. There are elegant stables for elephants and horses; the queen had a spacious bathing house that is a poem in stone with a grid-like pattern of descending staircases. There are banana tree plantations, palm trees, sugar cane fields and other crops scattered throughout the ruins. The poor live in villages where cows and goats roam; their day-to-day existence is obscure and they seem unaware of their past. They are perhaps more concerned with eking out a living, rather than with the splendour of kings long gone. In an age, this was a place where high thinking and fine living were taken for granted, a place where love and poetry flowered and there was as much music as speech, where love for their king, and a greater love for their god, became full. As masons repair various sites, one sees that neglect and poverty have replaced the opulence and exuberance of the past. It is sad to think that it became a ruin in the same century as it was built, and that the wealth of kings who were weighed in jewels, and who could sacrifice thousands of elephants, cattle and horses at a single yagya, were in the end only too human and had so very soon to succumb to dust. The ruins are as vast and grand as the villages that lie between them are humble. If one looks a second time, perhaps one would see that the people who live among the ruins also have great beauty and pride; their inherent simplicity propelled their survival where kings failed. The past is after all a part of their lives, and they were never separate from it. The temple of Shiva that still functions is for them like any place of pilgrimage. They do not marvel at the frescoed ceilings and painted columns of the central hallway because they live with them, and their acceptance of them goes deeper than outward praise. There is a sense of certainty of their roots in their unself-conscious silence. Perhaps it is something that only the unlettered can possess to that measure, for education could so easily dilute its purity in its headlong rush to progress.

Repose

Repose

Fishermen repair nets under palm trees in quiet unison, working over the fine surface with nimble fingers and not missing a stitch. Small pools of water have collected in the depressions on the beach. Three urchins play in the shallow water, splashing it up to the sun with shrill screams of delight. A vendor of snacks stands quite still by his goods and waits for business, beside the cart that is a rectangle on two circles. On waves further down, dark children bathe gleefully, jumping between the foam, their teeth white as the waves as they laugh. To a side, three fishermen row a catamaran into the water; it bobs in the tide, and the men rock rhythmically in it. A thatch roof café is raised on stilts over sand. The light of the late afternoon flows around the head of a girl drinking juice and on the shoulders of a boy. The light comes from the green-blue sea and it will be another hour before the sun sets. A catamaran on the sand is piled up with rope and rags and a crow perches upon its bamboo flagpole. The wind lifts the crow and flutters the rag flag; it seems abandoned like the other vessels all along the stretch of sand. There is one down the beach and a couple sits upon it, talking as froth spreads under their feet. By and large, the catamarans seem to lie there without motivation, their day's work done, and in their idleness, there is ease.

Then, through all the relaxedness in the air, it happens. Hordes of fishing people emerge out of the strolling and sitting crowds as if they have been sifted out suddenly, like grain from chaff. They stride across the sand, carrying basketfuls of fish upon their heads and talking raucously as they hurry forward. They stop and toss the fish by a spin of the baskets overhead in a gesture that only they could accomplish with such grace and speed. Every one of them talks animatedly as they scurry about, men, women, old people, and children- all, and one wonders who among them listens to whom. The fish spill through the air like so many shining pearls, and soon the commotion is over as they go for more from the boat that has just come in.

The beach fills in the evening with people from the town, and they walk, sit or wade ankle-deep into the waves. The sea darkens. A red disc dips upon it immediately ahead, leaving a glow in the sky after it has vanished. At night the waves rumble and the palm trees sometimes rustle. One san walk along the beach for miles and come across droves of seagulls in the day and only a few bathers, or the occasional boy riding his bicycle over firm sand. The sand is flat, fine and white and the water is warm and clear and always has a voice. An artist has modeled Jesus out of the sand. At night it was destroyed by the rising tide and only the Shiva on the other side of the mound remained intact. It is only four days to Christmas. There are a few coins in front of the Shiva, and the artist is sitting under a thatch shed in the distance, too proud to beg. The fishermen are still at work through the night, hurrying back and forth with baskets of fish on the beach. There is always such activity when work has to be done. They will sit quietly under the trees at noon, waiting for the catamarans to come in from the sea.

A Fort of the Sea

A Fort of the Sea

In the afternoon, the sea inhales and water recedes a great distance, leaving acres of flat sand that slope imperceptibly to the waves. The incline is gentle and stretches so far that one wonders why the water decided to stop just where it does. How does it consider where its limit should be? Distance accentuates the flatness of the sea and it appears no thicker than a grey-blue string that tumbles over with whiteness to turn grey again. It wavers at the horizon as if to keep alive the separation of land and sky. The sand stretches so far in some places that it makes an illusory black line immediately below the string that is water. People move like dots upon it as if balancing on a tightrope that curves faintly above the shimmering sand. Forms on land evaporate into a colourless haze; hills and plateaus are only half there like haunting dreams. Clusters of faded palm trees throw a discreet veil over the nondescript town behind them. A tiny temple on the shore glistens white even in the shade of the sultry afternoon that gives each thing a glaucous nimbus.

The sand has become complexly rippled and between ridges, water has remained. As one walks towards the ruin upon the line of sea, the furrows at one's feet become deeper and heavier. It is as if the water has moved in all directions simultaneously; in some places, its touch is gentle, in others, severe. Sometimes it has gouged fiercely, and then, with sculptor-like snipping and chopping, delved both angrily and delicately into the sand. The water is never more than several inches deep and sometimes contains sharp-edged stones that are still untamed by its motion in the half-day labyrinth. Further away, the skylight makes a mesh of ripples over undulating ground. In places, the puddles are too low for the breeze to shake. The field that spreads for kilometers glisters, and the descending sun wrests stern shadows within its monochrome.

Tiny shell animals under the limpid salt water scuttle and amble sluggishly, and further shoreward, are embedded in the drying sand and glisten immobile as pearls. They are still alive in miniature pools and will have to struggle until the night when the tide returns to rescue them, and they are wafted effortlessly to the ocean like little throbbing heartbeats. Clams have stuck to stones long ago, and their shells alone have endured, fixed like a mutation of the rock in a vestige of the loving embrace of the living for the body of earth. Only a few sandpipers run over the vast plain and suddenly stop in their airy tracks at shallow puddles, only to dart forward again and take wing.

Three or four boats rest near the walls of the ancient fort as if they had been tied to that edifice by the thin dark line on the horizon, hinting at a half-real world. There are rocky reefs as black and as low as lava, and among them, silhouettes of gaunt fishermen with oars in their hands. A few hold up a net on poles that flutters against the glare like a gossamer web. The breaking waves are so far away that they cannot be heard until one ascends the walls, and even from there, they are a hush. There is only a dull, strange thud for there is neither complete silence nor a perceptible breeze, nor an emptiness to transmit solitary sounds. Perhaps that hush too is evaporating into the haze. There are faint voices from fishermen and blazing outlines of children playing silently on the sand, yet one can almost hear the patter of feet on the wet ground or the whip of clothing in the light breeze. Perhaps the air consumes those sounds in the same way that the reflections are sucked into the intermittent shine of that endless floor of either mud or watered silk. One is much too small upon that yielding surface underfoot, that is easy to slice, nick or shake into any other mould of one's liking. Its changeableness expresses welcome. It is so wide so as to become a blur far away, yet not for a moment does it let one forget its transience and malleability. It is there in the afternoon, and in the evening, it is gone.

Upon that ephemeral terrain, the fort looms all the more unreal, a numbed stronghold immersed in all that changes, like a thought that remains stubbornly while a seamless moat comes and goes, or a mind that is within grasp for a few hours, and then becomes splendidly aloof in high tide. Paradoxically, it is at the time when water recedes and when one can walk quite simply up to it, that it impresses one as being lost to a no-man's land between yes and no, to a twilight between what exists and what is imagined. It is a time when the air is charged with poetry. When water surrounds the fort and submerges surrounding rocks, it becomes comprehensible and prosaic. Its mystery only wells up when it is accessible, for when it is difficult to reach, it does not lure. One knows that one has confronted something entirely new in being able to feel this way at the spot.

Shells between stones are buried in rubble. Each is white with black markings, as if the reef permits no colour. Ramparts of the fort stand isolated from the rest of the ruin, the adjoining wall having crumbled. A red flag flaps on rocks indifferent to the grey sea against which it stands. There are thin poles on faraway reefs that had once been flags too, but have become a graveyard that the sea winds have transformed into a skeleton.

One makes one's way between rocks, stopping to collect shells and climbing over walls that lead to the courtyard of the fort. Grasses and shrubs have overtaken the building. Outside the arch at the door, a leafy banyan tree shades a prayer stone and an unused well, its branches climbing tortuously over wall stones and its bunched aerial roots swaying low on the dust, almost brushing the whitewashed stone and marked area of the shrine. Trees have rooted themselves between stones and sprouted green where there was only charred granite, covering facades with creepers and thorns. There are foot worn mud trails through grassy ground that have been singed in the sun. Small stone carvings of gods on the floor have acquired prayer and wicker stiles and the path leads to more open space and to a courtyard with a whitewashed temple at its centre, standing above grassy mounds.

The ruin is still a place of pilgrimage. It's sculpted stone lattice windows and walls are painted over in lime that destroys the work of sea-weathered gods, the bloom of lonely bowers, the rage of demons and the ecstasy of goddesses. A pillar has been overlooked by painters and has blackened in the sun. The minor shrine that stands to a side has received a wash of paint as well and is finger-marked with saffron. Grass, stone and dust lead to walls beyond the courtyard. The sea is an immense and flat body and very far removed, its uniform grey turning to white at the edges. Even where the surf rises and dashes against black rocks in a flash, there is a curious silence.

One ascends the crumbled staircase to a door and sees the strange voiceless sea and textured sands. Two whitewashed gods protect the worn doorway with sealed lips and beneath, the waves sweep inland in silence too, making a curve that extends for kilometres. A half-filled tank of green water is still and sweet in the heart of a ruin encased within a ruin sea. It is deeper into the ground than the sands and the salty lapping waves beyond the walls.

Families live within the ruin and their dwellings are overgrown with plants. Two brightly attired women chatter up the staircase by the hidden tank and carry splashing buckets of water homeward. The wind stirs tall dry grass and children play in the mud outside their doors. There is silence in the niches beyond the ramparts where the sea can be seen and even the lone seagull overhead wheels in silence.

The sea has softened hard edges on stones and bones. If one spots something on the ground, it usually has an intricate and marvelous form that has been shaped and cleaned unpredictably by salt water. The setting sun gives the puddles fire as the wind continues to lend them a shudder. In the chill magic of the changing hour, waves unfurl in arabesques, determined to come closer inland with every passing moment. They become wilder as the sun turns into an oval disc that drops into the haze and leaves a darkening grey all round. An old fisherman calls out to his son and together, they drag a boat to rocky reefs to find an anchor in the slow tide of the ruin sea.

The Glowing Limb

The Glowing Limb

Zigzag paths lead up to a semi-circle of hidden stone cliffs into which many caves have been hewn. The entire mountainside was turned into a dwelling for monks long ago, and took centuries to build. So hidden were they indeed that they took yet many more centuries to rediscover, and even then, it happened by a mere chance that they were found at all. Lightless halls are enormous behind pillars, and the only glimmer to enter does so through doorways to the caves. Chisel marks decorate the ceilings and wall sculptures. There are parts where the work stopped before completion, and these are primitive and almost brutal in their beauty, the labour still showing through in a way that it cannot do in the refined and finished sculptures. One sees how caves began, for some are just stone holes that have been marked out with chisel strokes. There are innumerable images of the Buddha in stone and paint. Some paintings are scattered into pieces and chipped beyond recognition. Where they are untouched, the colours are fresh as if applied only yesterday. Faces are magical, serene and extraordinarily beautiful; jewels shine and limbs glisten where time has not eaten the pictures. Flowers still bloom, petals as fragile as if they belonged to an eternal springtime, and all in offering. Eyes glow and lips are sealed; the music of musicians and bells on dancers are silence, and then, the edge of the mural has been consumed by the wasteful hand of the ages. The ceilings are geometric and ornate and painted in black and white, clustered with peacocks, fish, lovers, lotuses, leaves and bowers. There are some large stupas, and the light falling in highlights certain parts of friezes and gives others shadow. The painted panels by the monk artists of long ago are infinitely refined, even to their exquisite renderings of animals. An elephant rushes out of a pond and scatters lotus flowers in his stride; a monkey on a bull's back covers the eyes of the animal he rides in glee. There are fantastic birds, deer, cows, elephants, horses, peacocks and other creatures. The humanity portrayed is always youthful and of great beauty in limb and head, and is at the pinnacle of grace. People are portrayed in the setting of their homes or fields, in forests or battlefields, in palaces and temples, and everywhere, they exude human perfection. There is not a painted face that is not soft and hinting at a spiritual beauty, although they impress one as belonging to the world. The monks rendered everything in the light of their inwardly enriched worldview, depicting the Jatakas in which the previous lives of the Buddha are enumerated. In so doing, they describe also the worldly and the luxurious. They painted the lives of their times meticulously, yet do not convey even for an instant that they, as artists, were leading the lives of denial in ascetic austerity, or that they were fantasizing as they created, or even that they were living in a make-believe world. It is not so, for the monks' realm of the spirit seems to say that it sees beauty in the world as it is. In so being, it becomes a deeply evolved view. Love, wealth, luxury, comfort, power and beauty are represented, yet along with the enormous labour is an underlying and essential harmony. One can imagine the monk living in his humble cell, fetching water from the river below the cliffs and carrying on his lifework in the deep recesses of the hewn caves with the reflected light of a piece of polished metal, virtually of the same kind that the keeper of the caves now uses to show visitors the murals. The ancient artist was able to show plants and animals, street scenes and resplendent Bodhisattvas, bejeweled princes and exquisite maidens with rare delicacy. The compassion and knowledge of divinity passed from the artist to his frail creation in an intermingling of god and creature. His labour enriched his life so deeply that he did not crave for the possessions of the world.

The curve of cliff continues beyond the last carving and swivels above the muddy rivulet at the foot of the ravine. There was room yet for many more generations of monks to demonstrate an unearthly love for the teaching and person of the Buddha. This undying passion is expressed succinctly in one sculpture where the face of the Buddha from one side looks solemn in contemplation, from another side looks joyful in the experience of nirvana, and from the angle below, has the equanimity of compassion. One wonders, did not each monk who lived here in dedication to his divine teacher, also possess, at least in some measure, those very qualities as well? The stones and strokes of the caves are silent, but to the weary pilgrim, they do whisper of the world to which each of us can have access, even in this life. The silence underneath the whisper persists nevertheless, and the rock facades that rise above the caves know it, the trees above the rivulet know it, and the low trickling water too breathes this agelessness.

There are ruins along the way into the fields that are green after the rain. Cow carts laden with bristling grass pull against the backdrop of hillocks and plateaus, driven by colourful villagers. Farmers are gathering hay to last the year; there are small white mosques on top of the hill, and one goes past them to the caves in the mountainside. They form their own spacious enclosure, and wear a thick monsoon coverlet of indigo clouds.

There are ethereal waterfalls against stern lava; cascades that sweep the stone as delicately as the final chisel strokes that centuries ago shaped the gods of the caves. Human hands working in unison over many years wrested, rather than built, the great temple of Kailasa, guided by the will of heaven, at each stroke doing away with rock and turning it to rubble. They gouged out each chip of unrelenting rock with the unswerving bhakti of seven centuries, to leave this imperishable testament of a soaring and aspiring human soul before the visitor. It is resplendent too in its ultimate physical shape, thickset, squat and of indomitable strength. It is a power that was won drop by sweating drop and belonged to a superhuman striving, withheld by miniscule human breaths that endured nearly a millennium to achieve a perfected end and final flourish. The towering human will, so obviously materialized in the sculpted sikharas, did not exclude humble monk cells that dot the courtyards, in its scope; some are scooped out in the simplest manner to provide a niche for the living of monks. The mountain wall face overhangs the magnificent temple like an ocean frozen for all time in its movement towards the monument. It is magically halted in its tracks by the very sanctity of the precinct, almost in resonance with the ancient myth of Kailasa being shaken by the demon Ravana, and which was to be quelled once and for all with a mere twiddle of Shiva's toe. This central story is repeated twice in the temple friezes, and once more in another nearby temple. The rock wall rises immensely high, sweeping vastly in a gesture of protection to the sikhara that is echoed five times in smaller replicas behind the sanctum. These five were in ancient times plastered white to reflect the snows of the isolated peak of the mountain in the Himalayas after which the temple is named. The sacred ambulation around the temple is long; its path echoed by the cliff that circles the monument overhead. The pilgrims that come in hundreds are dwarfed instantly in that largesse and their voices hushed to a pitter-patter. The infinite waves of carved gods and goddesses, chimera, demons and animals that embellish every façade melt before the elemental simplicity of the garbagriha that has a yoni lingam. The larger-than-life scale of the images is forgotten before the smaller size of the lingam that is wholly accessible. The darkness of the sanctum beckons one to move closer, even as the harsh sunlight outdoors tends to distance the images of gods from the pilgrim. The enormous scale of the temple-mountain must have appeared that much more awesome in the times when it was made, because even in a modern context, it shrinks the visitor with its primeval immensity. The rain falling on the temple is benign in its very slant. The first sensation upon entering the temple, at the juncture between the profane and sacred worlds, is one of immediate grandeur. One does not forget the decayed torsos of Vyasa and Valmiki at the doors, two celestial sages who worked their way in the heart of the world, and whose wisdom and example were an everlasting inspiration to the myriad sculptors, stone-cutters and masons who created Kailasa. For the great artists who made the temple, it became truly the centre of the universe; one can almost imagine a mythical tortoise underneath the temple, holding it aloft on its impregnable back. The villagers that come in prayer to the shrine need not know how to read, for the illustrative panels of the gods have instructed the unlettered ever since they were carved, in simple and unmistakable pictures from familiar stories in the Ramayana and Mahabharata.

A small Jain cave further away is elaborate with carvings of animals and the images of Mahavira. Tiny frescoes lurk beneath ceilings like hidden jewels and come to life under the candlelight of the keeper; there is a dancing foot here and a smile there, isolated in their survival through the passage of time. Here, as elsewhere, smaller temples serve to highlight the epic scale and accomplishment of Kailasa.

The road winds over hillocks, passing hamlets and villagers among fields. A fortress is set on top of a hill that falls conically down to sharp stone cliffs below thick woods. Tufts of grass have caught and grown in the fort walls. On ground level an orange minaret rises high against a blue horizon, and the small town is not too far away.

Steps by the Water

Steps by the Water

A group of brightly dressed women sits with children on a wooden platform over the steps, under a bamboo umbrella that keeps out the sun. A band of musicians plays as the barber shaves the head of a child to rotund smoothness. He then proceeds to massage the hair of another child before putting his scalpel to that too. Pundits lay out their ritual paraphernalia, the small vessels with holy water and coloured powders, beads and threads, flowers and bells. They await pilgrims who will sit on their daises to gain the blessings of the river. There are women with basket-loads of marigolds and rose petals, making leaf cups for the people who wind their way through crowded bazaars to the steps upon the water. Beggars eat gruel and some are very emaciated and leprous. An old man sits among terracotta pots and red scarves hanging from hooks. A woman dips cotton into oil and pats the back of a little boy with the wad, medicating him as he grimaces in pain. A cow wanders upon the steps and eats discarded garlands. In the shops above, a brown cow eats oranges out of a basket as the fruit-seller pushes it away. Boys shout gleefully and plunge into the river. One young man soaps himself white before taking a dive. The ghats span the whole length of the city upon the river; on the other bank, there is nothing except a barren and sandy stretch. A few boats are grounded on the crowded city side. The dead are cremated at a burning ghat where fires smoke with herbs and fragrant oblations and are bright orange in the evening's dying light. There is noise and singing over loudspeakers that have been mounted on the spires of temples. One deserted temple is half-sunk into the river and is at an incline. A hundred year-old priest has spread his cloth among utensils and rests under the shade of a tattered thatch umbrella near the crowds. Men wash their clothes, beating shirts and lungis upon the steps. Women are swathed in wet saris as they come up from the water; the wind fills the folds of their garments and stirs the dust upon the floor. Women in gold and silver sequins glitter their way down with infants crying in their arms. A boy sells wooden toys and looks at his customers as they play with sticks and rattles before deciding to buy. A rickshaw puller stops at a shop to buy chewing tobacco, saying that it keeps his mood going fine for the whole day. Boatmen make rounds, trying to get people for a joyride along the ghats. They persuade one by saying that the buildings are quaint and loom large on the waterfront view. A bald man rubs his head and dips into the river. Many people in the city begin their day at five in the morning with a bath in the river, and sometimes sip the water too. Babies are plunged into the water and come out screaming. Hundreds of pigeons flee a building to wheel briefly in the air and then return to their roosts. Buffaloes are led down for a bath, and lie like black stones upon green water, their heads surfacing occasionally. There are dozens of swallows above the burning ghat that is distinguished by its fires and piles of wood. Monkeys play the fool at a maroon temple and bathe in the cesspool below it. Little children receive marks of vermilion and sandalwood paste upon their foreheads. An aged pundit sells butter for lamps. Another pundit has lad out the vermilion powder, bowl, a plate of rice grain, a mango, two pots of water, a small vessel of flowers, incense, a mirror and a comb. Women carry leaf cups of flowers to the water. A young boy gets a haircut and then examines it in the mirror. Women cook rice over a twig fire. An old man in a white lungi and sacred thread carries a brass pot of water. A woman soaps a crying infant. A drummer leads women to the water; soon, another drummer appears and rivals the former with a faster beat. Temple bells ring. A goat nibbles at a priest's wares and is chased away. The priest brings a stone upon which to grind sandalwood. Men dry their clothes by throwing them on wickerwork umbrellas. A fat woman rubs herself on the steps for a whole hour. A boy bobs in the water using two oilcans as floats. A man does yoga on the steps. Five cows stand perfectly still in the middle of the crowded marketplace. Saris are spread out on the steps to dry. A sparrow pecks at the rice grain among the priest's objects. Vendors sell sweets upon large trays balanced on their heads. A pundit asks one to get up from the steps and go elsewhere as one's being there has brought him bad luck: he has had no business since one sat down near his dais.

A Serene God

A Serene God

There are hundreds of pilgrims at Matangesvar on the morning after Shivaratri. Some have even come in the humblest way imaginable, crawling on all fours for many kilometers. In turns, all the women in colourful saris ascend the steps of the temple, and they are followed by the men who are in shorts and bare-chested. They all carry small vessels of water from the pond for the blessing of the deity. The name of god is on every lip; the men shout it out, and the women chant together. Soon they have their darshan and leave, making room for more people to come. By the afternoon, the temple is all but deserted, and an archipelago of idling and yawning buffaloes overtakes the pond nearby, with a few urchins looking to them from the banks.

There were once eighty-five temples, but only twenty-five remain, the rest having been destroyed by vandals and heretics. They still bear testimony of human striving and perfection, and inspire the millions that visit them from all over the land. All the figures sculpted are in their various moods, poses, and moments, are caught unawares doing mundane things like their toilet, at play or while making love. They depict people who chanced upon a sudden realization when moksha was bestowed upon them as they heard the passing marriage procession of Shiva and Parvati. No matter what they were in the midst of doing, there was for them at that moment, complete liberation from worldly bondage; this was the gift of Shiva. The gods make love for an eternity in the stones of the temples in ecstasy, innocence and grace. Liberation is at the very soul of divinity, and humanity is given its darshan. The Chandela kings who built the temples showed longing in all its forms, in frieze after numberless frieze, to point to the emptiness and futility of desire. In looking at the temples, the pilgrim becomes saturated and can gain freedom from the very idea of wanting; in the witnessing is liberation. The discerning eye goes from layer to inner layer, and outwardly from level to higher level until the pinnacle of the sikhara is reached, the last mountain peak before the sky of freedom. Each desire is lived out, burned and gone beyond to reach inner peace. It is a final cave of darkness that one ultimately reaches, to the garbagriha that mirrors the nothingness of the Absolute, in the heart of searing light and heat. The formless within the womb is eschewed from the most ornate universe ever created by human hands. The persistence of the multiple has led to the singular, and sensuality has found completion in serenity.

Past the tiny roads where cartfuls of singing villagers return home, a temple nestles far in the fields. The rickshaw ride leaves the contemporary world behind; there is an empty road under the overcast sky and the air is fresh. Behind one, there is gold under the grey of threatening clouds. It begins to drizzle gently, and in the intermittent breeze, ripe wheat fields wave slowly, still golden and dry. The road inclines up to the small hamlet. Villagers pass by on their bicycles and walk on the flat land. A goat bleats and is lost among the shallow pools left by an earlier downpour. An eleven-foot Shiva has stood in his sanctum in shadow all day, but is now ignited by the light of the evening in the last rays of the sun. This has been the only light upon him for hundreds of years, apart from the tiny oil lamps that are lit in front of his image by the priest. He is unseen and magical, and unmoved by the wind that now stirs dry leaves in the temple precinct. The village children dawdle at the gate and beg for a coin or a pen; the Vindhya range behind the temple lights up biscuit against an indigo sky. The old rickshaw man pulls his vehicle through the fast wind with difficulty, and one returns on the village road once more. One takes a last look at the temple from far: a rainbow has arched high in the sky and ended spilling directly on to the sikhara of Chaturbhuj, as if that were to be its final home. Even droves of parrots flee the peepul trees enchanted, and the evening is slow in turning dark. A temple has been touched with the arch of an all-seeing god, and has poured itself in calmness at the feet of the divine being that rests within, bathing him in all seven colours of earth.

Above, an airplane takes off in flight, zooming enormous, and for the moment, belongs to another realm. One is sure that the world of the village temple also exists nevertheless, though of less admittance and untouched by modernity. Its charm and dignity are intact, and perhaps integrate into something much larger than what we call progress.

An Island of Prayer

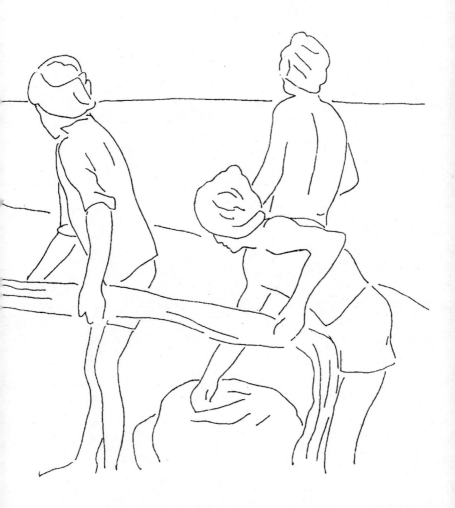

An Island of Prayer

Among the drab passengers, there is a magnificent villager who has squeezed his way through the small door, and taken a seat on the bus up ahead. Although he could not be past thirty-five, his face is dark and deeply wrinkled. He is tall and thin and his frame lends him grace and elegance. He has not shaved for a week and his large deep-set eyes give him a slightly ferocious expression. Under his turban of thick off-white cotton is a brass ring in one ear. His shirt and vest are off-white too, bound tight on his torso; his bony shoulders stick out and are very angular. His white dhoti is tied at the waist with a cord, and he is barefoot. His limbs are ebony on white folds of cloth and on each arm he wears broad silver bracelets. There is a cross-section of people on the bus, but the villager's newly washed clothes give him a dignity that is apart. There are families with young men and old men who carry small packets. Two boys turn on a radio that adds to the cacophony of grinding wheels and blaring horn as the bus moves. When it stops for refreshments on the road, there are

marvelously dressed villagers, red turbans and shawls glittering upon
dark skins and white clothes; upon their poverty is a festival. A few
monks in saffron mount among the throngs of ordinary looking people
who are returning to where they come from.

The road is narrow and winds sinuously through villages and fields.
The sea is not too far away and makes the air fresh and the countryside
lush. There are sugar cane fields and palm trees; often the fields are
bare, having been tilled to lay new seeds in the brown upturned soil.
Tractors, trucks and bicycles ply the road, and open carriage scooter
taxis hung with bright tinsel that make for curious transport are
stuffed with passengers. There are bullock carts, and sometimes they
have been decorated as if for an occasion. The bullocks have
embroidered cloths over their backs and carry women in red clothes
and men in scarlet turbans who chatter among themselves. A few
women have stoles on their heads and glitter with heavy sequins.
Their bodices are backless and mirrors glint in the folds of their
clothes. The men are often in white and their ears are pierced and
weighted down with silver and brass knobs that look like miniature
parasols on top of their earlobes. The bus goes over a bridge, and
below, on the banks of the river, women are laying out bright saris to
dry in the sun. A truck stops and the driver alights to fill his radiator
with the water, unconcerned about the silt it contains. A few small
temples stand behind the road in a village on the way. An ancient
Banyan tree overhangs pools of brackish water. Pigeons perch on the
domes that have been whitewashed several times and have a strange
patina, and the deities are ensconced behind bright cage doors. There

is soon a haze in the air that indicates the proximity of the sea. An island stretches upon the last line of vegetation beyond which a frayed line of palm trees hides the sea. The island is clearer as the land becomes more level and is distinct from the mainland, separated by salt fields. A small town in white and grey is set low on the horizon like cubic dominoes, and a dark monument stands out from the sparkling overall pattern. The road leads past a bridge and check posts and swings beneath palm trees. The town lies on a mild incline past stonewalls. Traffic consists mainly of bicycles and bullock carts upon the solitary island road. The air is balmy and there is no sound from the sea that gleams with the placidity of a lake, spreading endlessly behind the land.

The fort is at one extremity of the island, its walls dark and strong against the grey sea and hazy sky. It is an empty ruin; the few armed keepers at the gate wander to the enclosure within, guiding visitors. They lose interest in their chore soon enough and allow people to explore unaccompanied while they return to their post to smoke beedis under peepul trees. Canons have rusted and gathered patina over their iron, and there are mounds of large stone balls near them that have also been transformed by exposure to the salty air. The spacious enclosure is grassy and dry, with small buildings, churches and chapels. There are steep ramps to higher levels leading to a lighthouse from where the view of sea on one side and town on the other is splendid. The water is not rough and waves seldom break into open surf against the crumbled foundations of the fort. A prison, long out of use, stands in the water like a half-sunk submarine of granite, and has a nonfunctional lighthouse upon it. This monument of rock was a part of the fort that had been flung out to sea during a natural disaster, and managed to stay above the water. Large fishing boats glide to it, and seem to play with its edifice, not venturing too near, but stationing themselves within its proximity. Behind, another island that is separated from the mainland glistens in the haze with clusters of walls and windows. There are tiny silhouettes of people upon the fine beach that break the ordered geometry of the township's façade. The sea here is so shallow that people wade knee-deep in the water, almost up to the stony submarine. Waves lap gently on the sides of the fort where the stone has withered and become mottled. Walls still stand firm. The sea seems to return chips of stone to the fort, transforming their edges and giving them holes. The sandy stretch at the base of the fort is smooth and ridden with crabs. The sea is a moat around the monument; along the back wall a huge crevice has been dug to complete the passage of the moat. Shallow seawater ripples over textured sand, bringing another pattern to the curiously marked rock: golden ribs of sand show through the salt-blackened surface. The land is rocky up to the edge of water, scarred with lichen and green with seaweed; it is dry and bare, and does not throw up shells or sculpted stones, but rather, thorns and bleached twigs. Crabs feed off the slippery, mossy rock upon the very edge of the water.

The walled town is immaculate even in its poverty. A warren of paved streets has two-tier houses on both sides, and there are no trees or cars. The narrow paths permit only bushes to grow in the courtyards, or only bicycles and scooters to enter. Stray dogs bask in sunny spots, people squat outside their doors; at this time of day, the streets are empty and give the impression of an abandoned or sleepy town. There is comfort in its silence, and small groups of children playing marbles in alleys bring laughter and shouts, yet reassuring one of the ease of the afternoon. Doors are often brightly painted, their rusty hooks padlocked, and windows are shut behind heavy metal grills. It is poor, but clean and quiet. A door reveals a small tailor shop, or a cobbler, or silversmith, announced by gaudy signs, and then, along the whole street, doors and windows continue to be shut. A head peers over a small balcony, and there is a stroller or two; sometimes, music from a radio emanates from a room. That too, like the fluttering pigeon or the whelping puppy, succumbs to the undercurrent of contentment. Some the houses are old and need painting. Window grills have rotted, and vie for attention with the more obvious showy facades and painted floral pillars. Turning one street and entering deeper into the maze, one confronts a tempera mural of bunches of flowers and riders on horses that is faded for the most part yet exudes a quiet charm. Out of it unawares, one passes a school compound and a riotous bouquet of noises floats to one quite suddenly, replete with whistles, shouts, screams, laughter, and even the tinkle of bicycle bells. Sunlight falling on women lights them up brightly. It gives the backdrop of arcaded shops and grocery stalls that are further ahead a dull shadow that hints appropriately at their lunch hour closure before the activity of evening resumes.

Through an arched doorway, the road leads past dry landscape, shrubs and tiny villages to an incline where palm trees grow thicker. There are huts and fields under slender trunks, and leaving an abandoned building on top of a hillock, the road continues to bare mud fields to the island's edge. A bland sea is visible in the morning sunshine. A small square monument flutters with a delicate flag, and there is a lone boat, rocking gently on the water like a long black amphibian. The bay is a perfect hemisphere blocked by crags, and the sea fans out beyond it in both directions as far as one can see. Only palm trees stand upright and alone upon the water, and further inland they shade villages in clusters near the beach. A fine rim of white breaks in a circle on to land, unstitching itself into foam that falls in a thud to silence and revives time and again.

The village fields are close to the water, where sandy beach becomes shrub and palm tree plantation. A small farm with green fields nestles under the trees. At one end is a fresh water well upon which the farmer is at work. He waters his fields by turning the wheels that plunge clay jars into the well. They are pulled up to empty themselves in a stone basin. The spokes, pegs and wheel are of unevenly hewn wood, but the hub is shiny and perfectly lathed upon which the whole works well, driven by two oxen. It is an ingenious device of immemorial design, made simply of poles and sticks put together on wooden hinges and tied together by ropes. The oxen are tethered to a pole that moves the central hub and wedges its spokes into another upright wheel, parallel to the one that carries the jars that are brought up, sloshing into the basin to continue down the narrow drain to the crops in the fields. The eighteen jars are cracked at their rims and they surface like wet pumpkins, only to go down like empty gourds. The sticks of the wheel are irregularly made and held together stubbornly by hemp knots; jars are tied by finer rope like lumps on a bicycle chain. The small circle the oxen take is soft with mud and also uneven, so that each time they turn past the waterwheel, their pace quickens and the jars overturn with more verve. They are a fine pair with bells on their necks and macramé bands; their eyes are clean and wet and horns shine. The farmer positions himself upon a pole behind them and his foot rests on a string hook. Even in midair, he is comfortable and can speed his beasts as he smokes amidst splashing water. There are sounds of the wooden machine turning like a crazy symphony of wind instruments, topped with the tinkle of bells. The sounds rise high enough in the air to mingle with the consistent slap of waves not too far away while dry palms rustle in the low breeze. The three wheels, moving against mud and stone, wobble and creak, choke and wheeze, grind and squeak, and the water in the pots squelches and splutters and the whole creates spherical rhythm; one can move around it, and the sounds vary accordingly. Each afternoon, the farmer smokes on his merry-go-round, working on his fields, and making music.

The sea is cool; the sands burn at noon. Waves are tiny and the sea looks like a large lake, because of reefs. The sand is powder-fine, and rocks upon the beach are green with seaweed when the tide recedes. The moon rises like a disc of deep amber that dissolves in the luminous sky, shedding layer upon layer as it rises to become honey. Strange palm trees have clusters of fans-shaped leaves at the end of branches, and an orange coconut fruit that the boys of the village gather to sell in the markets far away. Everything has a miniscule fineness and an intricacy that an open, raging sea and an endless terrain of beach could never permit. The unseen stones underwater have checked, timed, and controlled the appearance of each thing upon the scene to its proper limit. The stones themselves surface only where the land ends and rise in cruel crags several scores of feet above the sea. They are fiercely mottled and holed, brutally scarred by mineral air and slowly beating foam. Stars are as limpid as jewels until the moonrise, and then their beauty fades as the sea takes on a shimmer in the quietness pervaded by the night. The cool sand resembles snow and the air is chill, but there is only a gentle breeze, not the wind that an open sea would bring. Small white birds cluster upon the flattened rocks and step back upon the incoming waves, and are soon gone. In some areas, the rock is a dark unrelenting mass that is ferociously eroded. The sea tosses up tiny crustaceans, pebbles, string and clumps of seaweed where the tide has been cornered by the rising rock. Where the beach is open, it is smooth, dry and without shells. Only rarely does a shell or stone shine pearl-like on its flat surface. Crabs too are tiny and have made homes in the sand, surrounded by a spray of ball bearing globules into which they dart unerringly. Patterns emerge from their clusters and reveal wet sand a millimetre underneath the dry crust of sand.

It is windy by the cliff and the sea has a habitual fury that has lashed the crumbling rock for millennia. The inflowing water has created caverns, leaving behind salts and turning stone to sand. The water flows shallow on reefs and waves swirl languidly over flattened stones. The afternoon sun gives the rock a stark chiaroscuro but is gentle on the water where it glitters. The sun is bland and benevolent, and falling surf makes no shadows. The pearly spray dashing upon crags is lost instantaneously.

Climbing the cruel rock, one sees that poor grass has taken root in the sparse soil and turned to hay. There are nests of birds among thorny bushes. Upon the stone, a chunk has been cut away to make room for a tree that has burst into a million green leaves, beyond which the sea spreads with a familiar heaving. The horizon is a blur of two blues upon which the sun spills sequins. Salt from the waves has taken refuge in the many holes of rock and hardened into a glittering white film. Small colourful birds twitter over the crags and a lone white crane swoops into shallow water, chased away by a dog that returns to lie in the sun. There is only stone upon those toothed crags; sometimes the dust permits grass and shrub to take root. In one place there is a small magenta flower, hidden among the holes. It is ablaze even while concealed in the shadows. For a moment, one wants to bend down and pluck the solitary flower. If something can grow there, one thinks, it must be very rare. And then, something makes one's hand stop; once plucked, the flower will become ordinary. It is the rock that makes it so precious. Has one been fooled into believing that the flower is so beautiful and rare? Is it true that nothing of perfection can grow on the scarred rock, because it has resisted nature too long and too thoroughly? Is the flower there only because the rock dared to exist? Would it have no life without

189

the vast body to support it, its beauty there because of the forbidding loneliness the rock knows? Are the flower and the rock two interlinked facets of a larger entity? Has the rock in fact resisted death by the sea, and has its strength made it ultimately distorted? Is it in the nature of the rock to resist? One has not even bent down to the flower to smell its perfume. Has the rock been abandoned by the elements, or is it only human beings that keep away from it? The stone and the flower are merely being themselves, and the only perfume is the one of the sea breeze, laden with salt.

Boys lead their small flock of cows and goats past waves and under the trees. The animals are thin and gentle, like the people of the island; the cows with curled horns look at one timorously, with the sweet fear and placidity of docile creatures. The small goats are irrepressibly buoyant and antic even as they walk across the beach, while the elders look neither left nor right but pace sternly to the groves. Two or three children who are no higher than the goats come following in line. They carry basins on their heads and collect dung for fuel. The boat that has gone out to sea in the morning returns at noon and folds its sail on the bay. It will bob on the waves until the next day and lie undisturbed and unused. The moonlight lights up the sea around the dark form of the boat at night, and a lone dog ambles up to the shore to settle on the cool sand. The sun comes up over the water, as pink as the moon has been amber, and soon the day returns to brightness. The sun sets behind trees and villages so that the glow of clouds reflects on water, turning its surface silver and silken, the waves calmly lap sands and unfurl foam on land that is the same colour as the sky. The breeze too is gentle, there and not quite there throughout the day and night. Kittens purr on tables and puppies whelp awake in the morning. The twitter of birds rises suddenly above the sounds of waves and melts into other rhythms of the place. Cocks strut on mud with flamboyance, uttering shrill cries at all times of day. An old man sits on a bench, head in shade while his clothes are in the sun. His fingers are gnarled with the years, and his eyes are nearly blind behind foggy and cracked eyeglasses. Crows are sleek in the bushes and among palm leaves. White bullocks are at rest in the fields, and the brown ones are at work. Butterflies flutter over sand, against the line of sea. Things, creatures and people seem mostly to be alone, except for the child goatherds and their flock, and each day submits languorously to its expression of living, warming as summer approaches.

Coffees come floating in a moat of more coffee on saucers, and the kindly servant tells one that one can even be served after midnight: even if the food is not ready, he would get up and cook, and there would be dinner at any hour. It is an old mansion on the beach that has been restored and is used as an inn for travelers. It is clean and simply furnished, and is the solitary building on the beach. As one enters the arch on the road, a sign announces the rules of the establishment, the menu, and bus timings. Young nature lovers stay for a few days and move on; the inn is not rich enough to have interfered with the natural rhythms of the environment. On Sundays, picnickers overtake the beach with ball games and venture into the water. They leave no trace of their coming, having wrapped away

191

their refuse and parcels carefully. Further into the fields, an abandoned room once served as a customs' office, but is now a whitewashed ruin with the anonymous graffiti that craves posterity all over its walls: those are the only leftovers of picnics.

A kitten is asleep on one's bed, curled up like another tossed garment on the coverlet. The night brings another moon on the water, its fullness vanishing with each consecutive evening, making its rising appear later and later. Oil lamps are lit and throw a warm glow over the walls; along with the gently beating waves, one hears crickets in doorway cracks, stirring the night to watchfulness. There are so many things: bicycle rides over inclines on smooth roads to tiny villages past casuarinas plantations and desert ground that is faintly spotted with dark bushes and stones. The narrow road is usually deserted; only once in a while, women appear in bright saris carrying earthenware pots on their heads, walking against the sun, so that they seem to move in an unreal halo of light.

On the shore near the town, women with baskets and men with briefcases, villagers with bundles and bicycles, all pile into the sailboat ferry. It floats low and sideways over the water to the other island. The sail is not used, but flaps in the breeze like an oversize pennant, stained ivory in the early morning light. On the other shore, the passengers alight and climb on to another boat. A thin wooden plank has been set on the edge, and the jump one takes gets one's shoes wet. The boatman chats while he accepts a coin for the ride, and one passes people squatting on the sand with baskets of fish, with children playing by their side. The small town is not fully awake at this hour, and there are only a few people at the gateway that leads to the mainland. Houses are tiny with latticed windows and balconies. Old wooden doors have been painted many times so that they have a lumpy veneer, and the plaster on the walls also has worn thick. A bus leads through villages, and for a while, the sea can still be seen. It is soon left behind and will become slowly forgotten. Tall leafy trees replace palm trees, as if to seal the scene that is left behind, and the ordinariness of the day overtakes one in moving on.

The Burning Turbans

The Burning Turbans

The water of the lake sparkles clean as wind gives rise to myriad waves. A natural island has a ruin temple upon it, its courtyard crumbling among the wild grasses. Bougainvillea and temple trees sprout flowers and pigeons stud the ruin like grey stones against a bland sky in the dying light. A palm tree sways in the breeze and its fronds rustle in the quiet evening. Pigeons take flight and there are sounds of other birds as well. A faraway island is clustered with trees and a lone building. The hills in the distance turn from dark grey to lighter shades until they merge with the sky. A palace atop one hill looks very much like an extension of the rock upon which it is built.

The only sounds to reach so far into the lake are natural ones: the birds, the breeze in foliage, the lapping of water. All this gives it a timeless tranquility. Ghats in the distance rise in balconies and pavilions and marvelously arched arcades between big Mango and Banyan trees and appear as a complex pattern of pale cubes. People bathe on the steps and women do their washing while young boys dip and splash and the elderly perform yogic exercises. Upon the water, a tiny pavilion on a tree-studded island is silent and empty. Lights are beginning to be lit and do not sparkle yet. At this changing hour, the sky, earth and water turn from grey to sepia, consecrating their all to the colour of dust; in such a place there is no haze but only clarity. Goats upon a terrace look out to the shore and below them women sit gossiping. Bright curtains flap upon windows so tiny that they would only permit one head to peer out of them at a time. A palace rises high and strong upon the heavy plasterwork of a creamy white honeycomb and has more windows, jutting terraces and pavilions and ornate domes. The darkening light brings ease upon faces and quietness to their gestures. The ruin temple that affords this view of a patchwork of many styles of architecture thrown together is away and devoid of humanity. There are only fish in the clean water and birds among its broken domes. In being apart, it assumes peacefulness. Its flowers are fragrant in the still air, and one forgets that the unkempt ruin is unused as it acquires another quality in that magical moment of day. A prince of long ago spent eight years here in exile, upon ever-rippling waves under the shadow of hills that appear to be flat and made of torn parchment, in contemplation of his kingdom. The strength of the city was far away, and its people lived beyond the façade of plaster, sometimes coming at their windows like so many specks, but no more. The magnificent plateaus on the other shore were perhaps more real to the prince and silhouettes of trees on that terrain may have seemed like cavalry stilled forever in its march across an unrelenting horizon.

Under the dry hillocks and by a temporary rainwater pond, an old Shiva temple breathes of another era. It is a small jewel that has become a ruin in the most gracious way that is possible for a monument to do so. It is so tiny that the devotee in one clear sweep can absorb it, and its proportions do not fail to impress one as being altogether human in their scale. The delicate carvings of the gods and their embellishments are fifteen hundred years old, and the foundations that remain of surrounding shrines, though completely crumbled, only add to the temple's isolated charm. Its existence speaks of the beauty and endless wealth of a land where one can still chance unawares upon a perfect masterpiece that is unknown and unsung and almost unrecorded.

Away upon the road that leads to villages, there is another temple site that is by contrast much visited. It is a clutter of closely placed shrines within a very restricted enclosure, and its very lack of space lends it great ambiance. The temples are medieval and of brown granite, but the floor that binds the whole complex together is of a modern design, of black and white diamond slabs of concrete; the contrast of the old and the recent gives it unique appeal. Turbaned retainers of the temple sit in the sunlight with bristling mustaches and white dhotis, bringing life to the small monuments, alongside the brightly dressed women who come to pray.

Further into the villages, there is a busy and crowded temple. It is visited by hundreds of colourful villagers and is decorated with frescoes of ultramarine elephants and red horses, golden tigers and bright maidens. Pilgrims swarm at the opening doors and a sea of humanity seems to move, ablaze in every hue. They have walked long distances over green hillocks and dusty roads to the noisy bazaars where the temple is. They pass its triple arched entrance attended by pundits with mantras upon their lips, past the folkloric murals to their bright deity for his blessing. They are soon finished with their pilgrimage, carrying the prasad their god gives in the form of sweets. They go through the busy bazaar, and on to the buses that will take them to their homes, still mumbling their prayers.

The ruins of the distant fortress are vast and its ramparts enormous. There are temples and palaces, walled courtyards and pavilions, gardens and terraces; their blackened facades add mystery to them and patina heightens their magic. Seen in utter silence, their pleasure is enhanced, for when they were built, they probably were no great marvels of architecture but functioned for the protection of the people against enemies. Their setting, upon dry and deserted mountaintops, turns them into monuments of great allure. They stretch for kilometers, and that accentuates their splendour. The windiness of the morning is drenched in sunshine and this adds to the aura of the ruins; in the hot summer, they are difficult to visit and to live in, and yet, even in that season, they would retain their depth in solitude, their apartness at a height from the levels below that humanity habitually knows. Their grandeur among humble villages is perennial. The countryside that has led to the fortress is magnificent, and yet nurtures inaccessibility to those very walls, until one understands how it truly was the most impregnable citadel of the region. Age has spoiled the sites, yet they remain aloof, as if perfected by the very hand of time that set to turn them into ruins.

The sun spills a golden and abundant light; in this season when nights are chill and days brilliant, one easily forgets the long hot summer one has lived through. There is lightness in the air and even birds tumble gleefully in flight. A road winds up a green hillock, past yellow and white temples in the bushes. The bus passes further on the road that is bordered with whitewashed stones and turns down the hillock as if a precious gem is hidden behind the trees. There is indeed a gem, for around the bend is a sleepy little town that awoke one morning and found that it was ready for the mela. People have come from faraway sandy villages on foot or by cart, bringing with them cattle and camels to sell at the fair. They have brought twigs for their campfires for in the desert there is little wood to be had. They carry all the money they saved over the past year. When they look at the little things the shops sell, their hearts bounce, their faces break into smiles and there is happy chatter. The narrow and crooked streets of the small town are full to bursting with village folk. The turbans burn yellow and red on the men and tinsel glints on the dresses of the women. Girls buy trinkets and young men puff at cheroots. The shops are full of colourful food. There are neckbands and bells for the camels. A coin shines on the deeply lined palm of an old man as he pays the vendor of sweets. There are basketfuls of pink roses at the entrance of temples. A naked fakir sits ashen among his mantras under a peepul tree. A lake shimmers grey-blue and young men dip into it. At the end of the bazaar, where the sands begin, camels and cattle are there in herds. Groups of women in flaming clothes sing as they cross the sands, and carry bundles on their heads. Children chew sugar cane, balancing the long sticks on their fingers as they bite and discard the husk on the ground. There are prayers everywhere, even on the lips of the camel seller as he collects dried camel dung from the sand for his fire. Brahma dropped a lotus petal and upon that spot a lake sprang up. Then, there were fairs. The plains are dusty and there are sharp dry hillocks in the distance, all stone and all grey. What do people need except a little food a day, and a mela every winter?

They are the most colourful people in the world, and this is the time when they are happiest. They come in large groups, in families and never singly, walking over stubble-studded slopes, past temples, creating their own pathways. They stop at temples to pray, carry their belongings on their heads and move until they reach the town where the fair is on. They are old and young and men and women and well and ill and children and infants-in-arms. Every single colour is upon their clothes; it is as if they never touched anything that had not reached a pinnacle of intense hue. Upon their dark skins, those very colours are iridescent. The lake is skirted round with tiny buildings and steps lead down to the edge of the water. The lake is holy, the temples are holy, but the most sacred is the main temple of Brahma. There are hundreds of pilgrims going through those doors to take the blessings of the deity who sits brightly painted and four-headed under a canopy in the shrine at the end of ascending steps. The shops burst with people and eating-houses are busy. The barbers have no time for anyone who wants a shave or a mustache twirled. Crowds jostle for all the things from villages that fill the stalls; they buy, eat happily, sit and talk or lie around in the shade of scant peepul trees. The streets are full of dust with the movement of so many feet upon them. The villagers buy images of Ganesh, Saraswati, Lakshmi and Hanuman made of brightly painted clay at the shops where the dunes begin. On the sands, thousands have camped with their camels and lit their fires of dung to cook their simple meal, or to bake small balls of bread under the embers. The settlements go on for kilometers. There are visitors from the world over who evoke the curiosity of the villagers in much the same way that they as tourists find the people of the region interesting. A village circus has been set up on the sands, and in a field nearby, there are camel races. Giantwheels creak on rotation, and there are games and amusements for child and adult alike among the blaring loudspeakers on tents. The men have wonderful dark faces and are mustached and wear elaborate turbans of the brightest colours, white dhotis and short shirts. They have glass jewels in their ears and brass and silver earrings and necklaces. The women are covered in flowing skirts and veils that reach their ankles. Everything they own is upon their bodies, all the silver bangles and necklaces and amulets and the borlas that adorn their foreheads. They have donned their newest clothes for the fair. A peacock feather is wrapped around the neck of a child as he sits in the arms of his father. A beggar wears an enormous turban of tattered tinsel and strange clothes to attract money. There are lepers and cripples at temple doors who wait for alms, and sadhus in orange. A limbless beggar lies on the road covered in ash and moans while a parrot struts over his torso, and one wonders how he is able to be alive at all. For the villagers who have come from far, it is more than a pilgrimage, it is more than a market for selling their animals; for them it is the best time of the year, a time of festivity when happiness bubbles over and is plain to see. It is a time when hard times are forgotten and poverty banished, if only for a few days and in only spending a few rupees. The people have forgotten their harsh labour in dry fields. They have not needed much to attain to the happiness that is written over their faces and marvelous clothes. It overflows on to the crowdedness of the streets, and is there in the ebullient dust that rises high into the sunlit air, its gold spreading for kilometers over the desert and meeting at the vibrating nucleus of the small town. A woman dries out a sari in the sun, stretching it across the road under a tree. Nearby, sadhus sit in groups talking or resting. Old men walk to the centre of the town with the help of sticks in one hand and rosaries in the other. The flow of people to the town is constant, yet there always seems to be enough room to accommodate them. A man sits on the roadside with a kettle and a few cups and that makes for his teashop. There seem to be temples everywhere, and even tents have images where a priest sits and chants while women come and fold their hands in prayer. A man sells rings and postcards weighted down by stones, and cannot do anything about the dust that settles on his wares. One man's turban seems to be so tightly twisted around his head that it looks like a rope. Noisy buses stop at the edge of the town, but the camel carts are allowed through. Men in bright neckbands have tassels that hang halfway down their shirts at the back. A bevy of girls bargains over necklaces at a booth and some of them finger the beads. A yellow temple has high arches at the entrance, and hundreds of villagers pass to and fro as a policeman tries to control their movement. Stunted dwarfs sit with arrogant expressions at the door, expecting a coin. The main street of the town is very crowded, but as one moves into the bylanes, the dust and quietness assail one unawares. The road veers down to the edge of the lake where colourful villagers are having their bath. Peacocks upon an old wall are still as if sculpted, and when their necks move, one knows that they are for real. The lake shimmers silver in the light of the setting sun, and the houses upon it look small. If it were not for the loudspeakers, the twitter of swallows on the water could be heard. One hillock has a temple on its peak, greying in the evening light. At the lakeside, there is segregation, except for a few male tourists who have trespassed into the women's area unsuspectingly, and no one is particularly concerned. The tourists laugh about having survived the meals in the small hotels. There are prayers everywhere, and shops begin to be lit with fairy lights. A temple's walls are bright with mirror mosaics, and people ring the overhead bell as they enter. Cows push their way through crowds as well. One sometimes spots black veils, but that too appears as a bright colour in the bazaar. The busy street has been divided in the middle with bamboo poles, but no one seems to know which direction to move in. It broadens into a square, and here sit hundreds of village women and men in separate groups in all their finery. The women sing and the men smoke, and the porches above the shops are lined with people too. Further, there are minstrels, and a shop selling postcards of the gods does brisk business. The electricity fails, but one can still see in the evening light, and then the lights come on again, accompanied by a mass of sighs. Hotels have chapattis hanging on threads at their doors to advertise meals. Women buy aluminum trunks and carry them on their heads and the men buy wooden rakes. A girl has bought a cooking pot and balances it on her head. The crowds are silhouettes among the few trees, and further, camels are shadows on the dunes. People sit in hundreds outside the temple doors by the sands, and one immediately senses the openness of the place after bazaar streets. Animals are herded by the thousands, the young among them antic in their movements even at this hour of evening. The colours are soft after the brightness of the day. Campfires glow in the greys of the evening and all the bright clothes on the villagers have been vanquished by the oncoming dark. Drums sound and there is singing coming from the dusty plain below the hillock. People will just sleep on the sands by the side of their camels. The fires are too tiny to glow too far, but they will give the campers some warmth in the night and heat enough to make a cup of tea. The world turns to sepia and indigo, and dust mingles with the smoke from fires. Men light beedis that appear like tiny orange light bulbs in their fingers. The moon is nearly full and shines white in a grey sky. When they gather in the dark outside the temple, their tinsel still glinting in the electric light, and turbans still aglow after the light in the sky has fallen, one knows that their souls are as bright as their clothes and as untouched by the push and pull of worldly matters, as they squat on the sand. A grey-white temple on the shore has a maroon flag fluttering upon it. All around the lake, pilgrims have doffed their resplendent apparel to bathe in the silver water. They offer prayers in the dying light, and set afloat small cups made of dough filled with cotton wicks dipped in mustard oil. They light these tiny vessels and place them on flat leaves and with just a gentle push, set them into the water; there are hundred of them on the placid lake. The pilgrimage that began flamboyantly ends in a silent offering in prayer, as the moon turns to fullness. Soon the streets of the tiny crooked town will return to their habitual emptiness; the joy of innumerable people that was showered upon it for a few days will become a wistful memory.

Shrubs sparsely dot the rocky hillocks of the dry country, and keeker trees and thorny bushes do somehow sprout on thick golden dust. The empty and rough road passes a sandy hamlet with a bright walled temple under taut trees and leads to a small village tucked under hills. It appears abandoned, and the small houses and courtyards that line the cobblestone path are charred and half-ruined. A few families persist in living among them out of want with their animals that lie amid piles of hay. There are no shops; in the afternoon the village is deserted. The beige stone of the hills comes right down to the sides of houses and often forms an extra wall to homes. There are cows and a goatherd leads his meager flock through the street. A turtledove flutters over a tattered stonewall. An impoverished family lives among the broken arches of a haveli, their clothes and all their possessions lying in the courtyard. Behind, the pillared walls are black with soot. A dog lolls lazily in the bright sunshine but there is nobody under the vast Banyan trees that have spread their roots over the road and burst through stone slabs. The village wears an aura of strange indifference where people survive anyhow in quiet hovels with their emaciated animals. Taps trickle over the cobblestones and there is a persistent stoicism underneath the poverty that nevertheless compromises the obscurity and neglect that the inhabitants know.

The cobbled way becomes cleaner as it leads up to an arch that ends in a palace. To a side, a stepped passage reaches up to a rocky hill that leads to a ruin fort. One encounters a few villagers on their descent and there is a woman on the slopes, gathering brushwood. Goats nibble on thorny bushes, and as one goes higher, the village below appears as a bottleneck between the hills that culminates in the palace. The steps end before a small cemented platform where a man gives passers-by water from a spouted brass vessel. From here, a stony path leads steeply to the ruin fort. An old wrinkled man mumbles and turns the locks on withered wooden doors to permit one to enter. Grasses grow wild among the rough stone, and the view beyond the ramparts is splendid. Colours soften at sunset and everything is touched with gold. The walls of the fort have blackened with time and in the perfect silence of a high place, a bleached peepul tree seems like an appropriate sentinel. There is no wind and it seems as if every living thing has been halted in its growth by a hand one cannot see. The old man does not feel this at all, but just opens another door that leads to more ruins. Through another doorway, one comes to a hidden haveli under the bare sky, its square and archways of peeling whitewash breathing abandon, but also a contentment away from quotidian involvement. In its neglect has afforded it an unearthly peace; there is the presence of what might be understood and felt as gratitude, at having been left alone by the curious people who visit the palace, or those who live struggling to survive in the village or aimlessly roam the deserted hills that surround the region. There is a hole in the floor of the innermost haveli and a tank underfoot, upon which is a pail on a string. In so dry and so far a place, it seems miraculous that it should be half-full of fresh water. It is as if the relief of being away from everything has instantly solidified into an object resting in an unknown corner. It gives succour even in its anonymity to the thirsty and weary visitor, however rare he might be.

Before dawn, the full moon is still low in the sky, and the only traffic one encounters is an elephant taking his constitutional around a block of the city. The bullock carts one sometimes sees on those lanes are not about as yet and one passes night watchmen huddled over small fires outside the gates of houses. Winter, that time for which the city yearns through heat and rain, is nearing, and the fragrance of burning leaves, mingling with low-lying mist, is almost its quiet, quick-vanishing harbinger. The road, through suburbs and industrial townships, is empty and leads to open spaces.

As the moon dips transparently, the road fills sporadically near villages with carts and trucks, their grey silhouettes all the more static through the windscreen of a speeding car. Camels pull box-carts of hay, the frail bamboo frames of their canopies bobbing heedless of sudden parrots that flee the thorny keeker trees in exhilarating clusters. As light spills over the flat country, turbaned cyclists, their white shirts crisped against the wind, tinkle the road awake, and women, slender in bright, limp saris, walk upright, balancing three-tier earthen pots with perfection over their heads, only occasionally breaking their symmetry with a brass vessel tucked under their arms. Names of villages mark the kilometers and read like a new line of perfumes, perhaps more sonorous than the villages themselves- Balchari, Gurota, Seekri, Tumasra, Karman- anonymous mud hut sprawls nesting tranquil by tiny shimmering ponds. They are identical and unaware of time, and were one not a mere passer-through, perhaps seeing the transistor radios, trucks, bicycle repair shops and stray dogs would have changed the view of the mud walls, dust trails and wells, the old men and the shiny-faced children on rope beds, the turtledoves that warble too close to the car. As one speeds past, the easeful impressions do not permit a whole reality to appear, and for those moments one leaves modernity for another graciousness.

An old pond is full of brackish water, though still used. Steps and ramps lead down to the level of the water, and on one side a row of cell-like rooms is built on a terrace that has decayed. One climbs the crumbled steps past them to the muddy roof and one comes to a shrine, ablaze with an orange Hanuman. A pundit recites the Ramayana before the image amidst frail threads of incense and flowers, and as one looks past the steps, one sees men doing yoga. People begin their day by the tank, bathing on the edge. Nearby, boys scrub bullocks as they sink into the big green tub. Even at this early hour, villagers gather around a visitor; the pahalwans stop their bone-cracking exercises midway as they untwist to watch from a distance. The women abandon earthen pots, following the boys and elders who smile and gesticulate among themselves, brimming with curiosity. The youngest children in the group break the ice by ambling up to one, mock begging for money with a sparkle in their eyes. Further through the bazaar of tiny shops and stalls that jut incongruously on to both sides of the road, one reaches the gates of the palace. Its steel mesh grill is just being opened, and the sweepers are brisk with their brooms at the doorway and in the courtyards within.

The palace is a whimsical monument, and in its present state that is a transition between complete abandonment and becoming a skeleton of faded glory, its eccentricity is accentuated. Its half-ruin aura is like a frame that clings to the vestiges of a silk scroll that once hung upon it. Ruefully, one consoles oneself that the ornate and festive touches that persevere never really pertained to a masterpiece, even in their heyday; yet they compel a fascination, and one wonders whether the owners had one day simply left their realized fancy and relinquished it to pursue another royal whim. There seem to be too many keepers, as if the passing of the years have multiplied the descendants of royal servants, but kept their loyalty intact. There are always children, and stray dogs that become part of the scene. The fountains that had been splendid a hundred years ago are now defunct, their narrow rectangular pools now dusty, chipping dry moss and weeds. Of five hundred spouts, a few trickle nostalgically, making tearful puddles on the ground. The unkempt lawns have a casual abundance that twittering parrots, warbling pigeons and chattering children enhance. The main palace that overlooks the tank is still partly furnished. Tucked behind the main hall is a room that is regularly used by the keepers as a temple and has become dingy and fragrant with incense soot. The entire front face of the building opens out so that it becomes a large hall; three seating areas are set with sofas as plump as matrons, replete with curved backs and armrests, often on legs in the form of animal paws. Six objects, wooden banisters with cloth frills that resemble giant combs hang halfway down from the ceiling and are hand-operated fans that had to be pulled on ropes to swing back and forth, making a breeze. There are mirrored chests over foot-weary carpets that reflect outdoor light enigmatically; marble floors are immaculate. In one corner stands an enormous marble swing chair upon a pedestal, and a bed on an upper floor is as big as a pair of pool tables put together, isolated on its bell-shaped silver pegs in an empty room. A marble-floored dining room has a hairclip-shaped raised surface built eight inches off the ground and served as a dining area for banquets at which guest would sit in lotus posture. A thoughtful counterpart to this room stood on a level below, furnished with a large table and chairs. A chess room displays an empty board, as unfrequented as the rest of the palace, except by attendants who dust each thing lovingly.

Another building is now a half-ghost, festooned with several tinsel Christmas balls that are perched on the high ceiling more precariously than pigeons. Two stuffed tigers look morose, and between them a carved peg table props up a cutout daguerreotype of a maharaja gazing at visitors. The old turbaned attendant delights in showing off stray artifacts while he sparkles with tales of glory of erstwhile rulers, beaming with both pride and exaggeration. Ascending a brick ramp, one comes upon a sunny and bare roof that overlooks a cluster of apartments, terraces and bread-loaf shaped cenotaphs. An entrance chamber below the roof was painted with frescoes depicting the life of Krishna, and embellished with elephants and horses. From here, one could see that a family of villagers have pitched tent on one of the terraces; a woman is busy lighting a cooking fire as her husband breaks twigs and the child fans the wisp of flame between two bricks. The small town too displays the day-to-day chores of its inhabitants. It moves at bullock-cart pace, and that means something slower than walking on foot: there is time. The walls that circuit the town for eight kilometers have crumbled; the fort lies beyond the palace and the dry, flat country stretches away into a haze.

Activity centers upon the palace and in the tiny bazaar that is not far away. Swallows trill and circle buoyantly over the tank where boys jump from the high ramparts to splash raucously. Women on the steps whip and slap their laundry angrily while the ancients take cautious dips, their hands folded over their eyes in prayer. The line of shrubs and bushes is stern against the walls of the fort that seem to sink contentedly into the green moat.

Skirting village squares, the road leads to a fabled walled town, and one is again in open country that is at its most verdant at this time of year. The road is narrow and the car periodically has to swerve off onto the dirt track as buses and trucks bypass one, making clouds of dust that give the landscape a golden haze before it freezes on windowpanes. There are horse and bullock carts full of villagers, all dressed in the colours of the sunset and bunched like temple flowers as they wobble along, smiling and often singing among themselves. These roads are made for them, one thinks, they are not for trucks; even the bicycles are aliens. The landscape too is theirs, its incandescent white shrines, some no more than two feet high, these are theirs, and the tiny mosques with twin minarets tucked away in the grass, all theirs. For just a moment, the kohl-smeared eyes of children flash past, and their smiles linger a while longer on that road. Sometimes one can spot a triangle of geese flying low enough to be heard on their way to a nearby sanctuary, or sometimes, the air is rent with the shriek of a bird in solitary flight. Peacocks flutter past the road in the late afternoon, and one is not far from the city.

A Secret Hill

A Secret Hill

From the sky, the land appears to be bits and pieces of squares that are sometimes green, but mostly of mud. Villages are like microchips from the air. As one descends, cubes of houses become clearer, colours glinting among the plethora of white and beige, speckled with dark little squares of windows and doors. Here and there, a spire or pole sticks out of the pattern like a needle. Moving further down, the high chimneys of brick kilns appear and people begin to move like small dots; that is the way people begin, tiny and wonderful. The fields give way to tree-dotted hills that become greener as they go higher. There are terraced fields on hillsides and the snaky lines of rivulets and roads through warps of hills. Fields are like watered silk in the rolling expanse of hilltops. Parallelograms of tin roofs shine on slopes and purple shadows of overhead clouds appear stationary. White clouds float horizontally far above the land, and in the distance below them are huge brown curls of a flat riverbed beyond the lowest hills.

The hills become higher and barer. A grey-green river winds

through the sharp cleft of a valley. Hilltops have tiny houses perched upon them. The small aircraft hits air pockets and bumps onward. There are zigzag paths on the mountains below that are thread-thin and clear upon shaded green land. Hillsides are all scree on one face and thick with vegetation on the other. Grey outlines of other hills begin where the broad tree-lined valleys end. Sometimes the paths on hills are bright yellow, displaying mud. A stretch of snow-covered ranges begins behind clouds. As the aircraft begins its descent, settlements appear among pines over spacious hillsides. There are grey clusters of flat, horizontal huts on ledges of mountain that blend with the rocks, as they lie low on the ground. The aircraft follows the narrowing valley, pursuing its hollows deeper into the mountains, and it lands at its end. Villagers from the mountains have come from far to see the lone aircraft land, and then roar and take off into the air once more.

There is brilliant sunshine on the hills and in the bazaar behind the airfield, and it is crisply hot in the streets. The green slopes rise high, and frail wisps of snow are discernible on the highest blue ridges. Coolies in the bazaar wear tatters, and thin men carry bundles of twigs on their backs. The bus begins to fill with hill folk; there are old men with marvelous wrinkles and brightly dressed women with children in their arms, meek policemen and gaudy young couples. While they are finding their seats, the driver jumps into his own chair and turns on the radio full blast. The bazaar is full of a motley crowd and among them is a group of monk boys in maroon clothes who lounge to admire an army jeep while they eat peanuts.

The road follows the river that is full of rocks and has some islands clustered with trees. Occasionally there are people bathing in the river. One arrives at a village with shingle roof huts and one soon passes its tiny shops to open spaces again. The road winds upwards through the valley while the river roars below, still within view. The bus often stops to pick up waving villagers and then rumbles on, more full than ever. There are peaks in the distance, wide valleys and more small towns along the way interspersed with wheat fields and apple orchards. Soon, the bus halts in a noisy bazaar where the riverside road seems to end.

The bazaar is a formless tumble on both sides of the road. Shops have grown and squeezed themselves between older establishments, so that there is old and new, poor and prosperous in the same area. The road is full of people and hawkers with a few pushcarts; cars and jeeps horn through crowds. There are paint and hardware stores next to general merchants, a bakery whose fragrance wafts into the street, small teashops with steaming kettles, restaurants and more gaudy shops, and there are more shops on the first floor of the buildings. It is still a poor market, not as yet spoiled by the taste that the well-to-do shopkeeper so quickly acquires. Coolies squat on the roadsides to light their beedis, and the boy making popcorn briskly turns his ladle to make the corn burst faster over the flames. Policemen look here and there into the crowds, and the vegetable seller swats flies off piles of fruit and cabbages and old, brown carrots. Shops sell brightly knitted socks and sweaters and blankets, and other hawkers have opened stalls of trinkets and bangles on the pavement. There is noise and activity, and the snow-peak mountains that can be seen on all sides behind the bazaar appear distant and alien to this setting. A garish temple on the road is just another shop, its bright and ornate deity well lit and able to be seen by people in passing vehicles, and completely accessible. It is decorated with tinsel and plastic garlands and hung with tissue paper flags. There are small offices on the road and banks behind metal grills, and over to a side is a small park with swings, seesaws and slides, full of screaming and running children. The post office is tiny with a tin box nailed to a wooden pillar in the corridor. In the provision store next door, the keeper reads a withered old newspaper amid sacks of grain. There are quaintly and awkwardly painted signs everywhere, announcing various establishments, and looking past them all, one also discovers ragged prayer flags hanging limp across the road. The bus stand is on mud with no parking system at all. There are teashops here that seem to have survived the dark ages, but they are as popular as the more modern variety. A dry cleaning shop is busy with boys ironing clothes to hang on a neat line of hangers, and sweet shops are full of colourful food behind smudged glass panels. Young men hang around street corners and visitors sniff in fascination from shop to shop. People seem busy with nothing, even the women who haggle over vegetables and fruit, and the taxi men who seem to find no customers. There is activity during the day, and by the evening, the crowds thin out and the bazaar closes down, the pushcarts roll away, and the small town grows cold in the night and seems to huddle cozily to sleep.

The solitary road leads up the hill from the bazaar, passing hotels and houses on both sides as the trees become thicker. Rills trickle through grass, and villagers in their traditional attire replace the conspicuous and jarring visitors one saw earlier. There are women carrying basketfuls of grass for their animals and they chat among themselves as they go on to fields that border the road. They have not been won over by the plastic jackets and rubber shoes that are perhaps more practical, and which the young boys have adopted, having had more exposure to people from the plains. The villagers sit on stone stiles that mark boundaries between huts among piles of fragrant wood. Some lead flocks of sheep, asses and cows down the road, clicking on their tongues and waving sticks as they move their beasts onward. The road takes a turn and one hears the jade and milk river rushing below through the high trees, and then, another turn blocks that sound completely. The road soon ends and a mud trail takes over, leading on the mountainside to wheat fields and apple orchards.

The mountains are high and deep green with dense cedar that stand upright like a quiver full of arrows all pointing skyward. Beyond them are spectacular snows on sharp peaks that shine white in the sun, and beyond, only flat sky. The roar of the river can be heard in most parts of the valley, and is a uniform sound underneath the shrill cries of birds and the miniscule buzz of flies and bees. Waterfalls on steep cliffs tumble silently and the low wheat in the fields waves rhythmically in the breeze; the cedars that tower in the distance catch the breeze too, and rustle as their topmost branches sway gently. The strong morning sun dries out dewy fields and brings a glitter to rocks; in the afternoons, clouds invade the valley and there is a fine slanting drizzle that vies with the vertical solidity of the Cedars. Paths become instantly speckled with raindrops, and villagers upon them quicken their pace homewards past stiles and thickets. Tiny clusters of villages on opposite hills fade in the haze of clouds, their horizontal roofs mingling with background colours. A curious quietness descends through the faint patter of drizzle and the fragrances of a rich earth become distinct. Calves are tethered by ropes to logs of wood and even their bells are silent. Cries of birds too disappear, and strangely, the flutes one heard across the hills are also gone. Only the sound of the river persists in the rainfall.

Where apple orchards end, small wheat fields begin, descending the valley in irregular steps. A farmer drives two black oxen in one of the patches, tilling the earth and turning it up in huge clods. A woman follows him with a pickaxe, chopping the clods to finer fragments. The animals stop in their tracks every few feet, and the farmer hisses, shouts and smacks them with a stick. Slowly, the metal bit at the end of the wooden yolk delves into the ground, transforming its texture. The heady smell of fresh soil rises into the sunny air as another colour is added to the greens and browns of terraces. Beyond the fields, the cedars begin, separated by a sliver of rill that gurgles buoyantly down the slope. A rich dark viridian mass of spikes reaches upward, completely different in character to the fields in front of it, or the snow-covered peaks far behind.

Quietness envelopes one in going past the first trees in the ascent on grassy ground. The cedars are very tall and straight, and foliage from lower parts of their trunks has fallen away, so that the tops look furry and spread out. The humid ground permits a lush growth of grass and clover, and is dappled by sunlight. The afternoon sun beaming through branches appears more of a sparkler than a constantly shining disc, and has unique charm as it sheds a soft and intermittent light through the forest. In its shadows, the cries of mountain birds seem to hollow out, as if coming from very far away. The ground is littered with needles and along the meadows there are huge boulders half sunk into the ground and ravaged by moss. They are sculptural; the shadows playing upon the surface that the lichen and weather altered, now give them an added texture. The largest rock is in the middle of the forest, below which rainwater has collected into a temporary pond. The surface water is perfectly still in the unreal light and reflects the strata and curves of the rock, the straightness of the cedars and limpid air immaculately. As the breeze comes up the valley, or descends from the peaks, it too becomes transformed upon touching the enormous trees, creating a magical hush and a faint whisper that seems to speak of unknown things. A woman grazes quiet black cattle in the meadow, and somewhere deeper in the forest, a man chops up a trunk into smaller pieces with a shining axe while the perfume of sap impregnates the air as new orange wood appears upon each blow. Elfin children walk silently through the forest carrying schoolbags larger than the backs upon which they are supported. The rumblings of a truck as it winds up the hill can be heard far below, but this seems to belong to another world that can never become part of the forest.

In a shadowy clearing among the cedars stands a pagoda-like

wooden temple. Over the centuries, the planks from which it is made have weathered so evenly that from a distance, they appear metallic. The base of the temple is of whitewashed stones that sparkle in the half-light. Near the main structure is a small hut with shingle roof and walls of cracked mud. A small wooden door on the side permits entry only when one crouches. Outside, a brass tap is tied with a magenta rag, and upon a large rock that protrudes from the ground an empty brass vessel glows strangely in harmony with the trickle. There is a stone courtyard leading to the temple, made of irregular tiles that sink towards the middle. The façade is of raw wood, intricately carved with figures of the gods. On supporting pillars, skulls of antelopes and deer have been nailed and the horns have turned white over the years. A young boy stands in the doorway and is the keeper of the shrine. There is no light inside, not even a candle in front of the tiny icon that stands under a long slanting slab of stone that juts out from the wall. There are a few small flowers in front of the image that ignite with the light coming in from the open door. An unevenly rising floor is discernible in that light and is caked impeccably with mud. It is a sculptural surface that allowed the ground to remain as it was before the temple was erected. A hole in the floor is used for goat sacrifices, and a little away, a square has been chiseled into the ground and is full of ashes. Triangles of red satin cloth are slung around corners, shining in low light, and there are more rock ledges along the walls. Coming out into the open, while putting on one's shoes that were left at the steps, a bearded priest emerges from the small door of the adjacent hut, dressed in white with eyes set afire upon dark skin; he seems to be another figure from a half-enchanted realm.

The cedars appear almost stronger as one moves again among them. There is an ox skull on the grass, covered in ants, the teeth white and untouched and the bone brown and decaying. There is a grassy ditch with old clothes thrown into a corner like a magic spell. The forest descends sharply from the edge of the hill and one can see roofs of homes below the trees in the valley. On the other side, the slope is gentler and thin paths lead downward. Feet are trapped against exposed roots in trying to gain a foothold. Wheat fields shine past the trunks of trees and are green in the distance. Figures of villagers beyond the terraces seem enchanted and behind them, another forest begins among cottages and large rocks. Other hills lie further, and appear like dark blue outlines against the sky; in one corner, snowy peaks are enveloped in blazing clouds. The blue sky above is untouched by the capricious play of light and glows evenly. Coming down to a rippling rill that seals the forest off with its silvery thread as it meanders unknowingly and divides two worlds, one reaches open sunshine again.

The road follows the river for a while and goes into the broadening valley, leaving the thunder of the water behind. In going further, ranges are also left behind, and the view widens to permit another vast range to appear, its dark rock layered in the blazing white of fresh fallen snow. The sun is sometimes behind clouds and its heat is inconsistent. One passes large buildings to spaces with few villages, where wheat fields stretch up to newer mountains. Opposite ranges have clusters of blue-green trees that conceal bare crags; in a few places waterfalls rush down, their flying waters strangely silent from far. The road slopes downward around a hillside and another river can be seen. It is much like any other mountain river, brisk over rocks through grassy banks, its green turning to foam in a hundred places. The road turns again past a wooden bridge and the valley opens out. Children play near a brook that runs on the side of the road. An orange truck rumbles by, creating swirls of dust that rise languidly in the still air and obscure the road behind. Farmers in the fields till the soil and utter sharp cries to move their animals on. A large village appears, one too poor to afford enamel paint on wooden walls or cement on floors, and thus retains its old structures intact. The bases of houses are of mud-layered stones and the low first floors are of wood. The houses have small arched windows that are roughly carved, and often, corridors are supported on wooden pillars and sunken around the middle, so that they appear dilapidated and very used. Shingle roofs are old and crumbling in places. There are weaving looms on many of the balconies that seem like primitive wooden assemblages. No one seems to be working on them, the people having gone into the fields for the day, so that the homes look deserted. By and large, the inhabitants seem to lead an outdoor life, and to retreat to the warmth of their homes only after dark. The village rises with the valley in steps against the magnificent backdrop of sharply rising mountains. Apart from vacant children in mud-laden alleyways, there are few people about. There are stacks of wood and hay, and the stone stiles that border each house are piled high with purple twigs to keep the animals out. A white pony is tied to the pillars of one home and eats hay. Large lizards on the rocks chase each other in the sun. Three farmers descend the terraces with a flock of sheep that amble across the road, bleating and going all ways before being rounded up with sticks and cries. Colourful village women with bundles on their backs stop at a roadside tap for a drink of water and wash their faces. A solitary brick building is full of children squatting on the floor of the verandah with their satchels, slates and books, and a woman sits behind a desk and conducts class over their chattering voices. Small faces are bright with glowing eyes, and smiles are ready and spontaneous, their attention far away from their studies. Fields and villages continue down the slope until they encounter the river at the bottom. The other side of the valley rises similarly, dotted with small huts and fields that nestle under the high ridges. In the distance, a series of slopes tumble downward to meet other slopes, and the ranges become greyer as the eyes move further, and at the very end, a haze merges with the sky.

The river dashes itself upon rocks and does not care how it goes. Somehow it finds and creates banks through the mountain land, and the rocks it ruffles over transform it into a green and white body as if in sympathy with its spirit. Its waters are as cold as ice but more limpid, ever new. It seems as if it will always have the gift of newness and that the high snows will never stop their melting to give it more. It rounds the cruelest rocks but does not move them from their beds, and it sweeps twigs in its wild course that often get caught between boulders, wagging nervously in the splash of foam and torrent of water, becoming invisible and reappearing rhythmically. The river is youthful and runs through stony, grassy ground. A cedar forest has grown on its banks, roots of enormous trees desperately gripping boulders and mud in order to stand. The ground is lumpy and green; roots that are finer jut out over the grass like veins upon an old hand, crisscrossing in some places before disappearing into the ground. Tiny rills flow into the river, sweeping tall grass along. Donkeys graze and the paths up to the trees are strewn with needles. There are sandy banks by the river and in places trickling ponds have formed, so that their surface shimmers and branches trapped underwater wave pensively. The roar of the river subsides as one moves among the cedars, and stillness overtakes one. Snows have greyed as if in anger and there is distant thunder. The sky becomes dark, and one goes into the open once more to see it loom threateningly above. Roads and bushes capture the unreal light. The sky remains bright in parts, but that too is gone, and the valley seems to have fine gauze dropped upon it. Mountains become silhouettes and their ranges assume gradations of greys. Soon, the drizzle washes and subdues everything in sight, giving equally to all. Waterfalls numb as swirls of white cloud hang in the middle of the valley, stealthily overtaking hillsides so that new contours of terrain become apparent and trees are outlined individually. The furthest range of snows is blanketed in clouds as well, and below one, the earth drinks and apple trees sway in the wind. The uphill road is completely awash and water flows down its sides. A calf is drenched and its fur has darkened while its eyes are moist and shine placidly through the rain. Leaves and blades of grass take on a new clarity even as the voice of the river deafens and submerges the patter of the rainfall.

The stony path winds upward along the hillside and leaves the river far below. Village women are coming down, carrying large bundles on their backs, bent over as they take steps cautiously over stones. A three year old walks his way home and gives a quick smile, but is too shy to start a conversation. The village on the mountainside sprawls on both sides of the path that has water running over it. Dirt is smudged over wooden houses that are built randomly a little above the trees and are sometimes perched on sharply descending hillsides. Cows are tied to walls with fine hooks and eat hay, and on balconies, faces of little children or old men peer out of arched windows. Borders of doors are ornately painted in orange, yet otherwise the lack of paint gives the poor homes a dignity. A woman dries out grain on a sunny courtyard, and behind the stiles of another house, two children in rags play with a tin car. A man stitches a pink quilt in quiet concentration while another puffs at his clay pipe. Further up the path, the houses give way to the mountainside again and to the sight and sound of the river beyond the green slopes and cliffs. A man washes clothes on a scooped out rock where the brook meets the path, and a girl does the same on another similar rock up a little way. The countryside is enriched by water, verdant with shrubs that cling to the strong stone and soil and huge trees that begin higher on the slope. Going downward, one is soon on the uneven banks of the river that have narrowed slightly, being upstream. The snows seem not too far away but are inaccessible. A man carrying wood on his back walks up the narrow pathway to the village where he encounters more people washing on carved stones. Nature seems to become more fierce and unyielding in its purity where the path comes to an end; there is a sense of loneliness in seeing the overgrowth of thorn upon sharp cliffs that bar the way and cannot be crossed. In the evening, the sky turns a strange brown. A band of blue persists and remains a long time, even when darkness has fallen over the valley, an after image that glows enigmatically over the brooding outlines of hills. Rain slants in the sky over snows and pale clouds obscure mountain crags, fading them out as they stand black-brown and white like a brittle sepia photograph past the cedars. There is thunder and the sky erupts periodically in white flashes that bleach trees and hillsides in lightning. On facing mountains, tiny golden lights of oil lamps begin to be lit, marking out areas in the dark body of rock and tree, beacons of warmth that survive the windswept countryside.

The highest tips of trees sway in the phantom forest breeze while trunks remain immobile. Sunlight is faint and the cries of birds have been stilled. A circle of sky is dappled with clouds above the rain pond, and it stretches and contracts with the swaying of trees. The cedars have begun to shed needles and descend like snowflakes, their gold striking the gold of the sun. The pond is a little larger because of the night's rain, and the surface is no longer clear. A mass of needles floats upon it, moving imperceptibly. It is brown with weeds that cling to the bottom, and insects flit underwater. The surface too is full of fragile ripples made by tiny vibrating insects. Dragonflies with iridescent bodies and gossamer wings flick and hover, then settle on weeds on the pond's edges. The rock lurches above, mottled with moss and strewn with needles, and underneath its shade, white butterflies flutter among ferns. The breeze stops and the cedars assume their calm, unshakeable and vertical against the sky. Four waifs come to wade in the pond, goblin-like three year-olds who venture from the edge and find that the water only comes up to their knees. They soon go away laughing and chattering, and the pond becomes alone once more. A bird warbles in an enchanted language that perhaps only the forest understands. The amber water reflects the cedars with a shudder. On a path beyond, a little boy walks towards the hill, whistling. Three woodcutters appear burdened with their newly acquired load, and behind them is a woman with twigs piled into her wicker basket. The brass bells of the temple sound faint and uneven over the slope. Perhaps the real temple extends near around the pond somewhere and is not restricted to the doors that were built to protect a tiny deity. The temple is here too, and cobwebs that stretch nearly invisible across saplings and thickets have ringed in the path to it. They are perfect in their fragility and one hesitates to trespass and stir the spiders that sleep at their centers or break the fine threads that bind branch to branch. Heaps of flies swarm on dung under new trees and glitter metallic in the sun as they buzz thick over the tiny mounds. The far rumble of trucks or the shrill horns of cars coming uphill do not dissipate the enchantment of the forest. From nearby villages comes the bellowing of cows and large mountain crows swoop up to the high branches and let off abrupt cries. A small breeze carries the aroma of cedar and even the smell of a pond full of weeds and that of freshly chopped wood. People who come into the forest do not stay long; if they chance upon the charred bones of an animal in a ditch, they mistake them for something grotesque. Apart from the people who live in its vicinity, the forest is alone. Perhaps only the woodcutter who passes it every day understands it, yet once again, perhaps he does not know that he understands. In putting one's arms around the mottled bark of cedars, one knows a little of their peace and strength, and then, trampling crisp cones underfoot makes one see in a different thing in a different way. There are many wood clumps on the ground, cedars that have been felled. Perhaps the sanctuary that had stood even before the image of the goddess was placed in the temple will not last forever in its aloneness and abundance. As evening falls, the area of the pond becomes quieter, if that were ever possible. The water radiates a tranquil mystery and the light of the sky through the straight line of trees comes with the strangest quivering. The strata of the large boulder are reflected symmetrically in all their shades of brown and grey. The breeze and dragonflies of the afternoon have gone, and car horns stilled for the approaching night. Evening persists in pale new colours but will soon melt into darkness and into the silence of shining stars. On an edge of the circle of sky a frail half moon appears, fixed and white with the clouds, as if it had found a place above feathery clumps of cedar.

The river thunders fluorescent, and its roar has been heightened by the quiet of the night. Tall trees are black against the luminous sky and the moon appears behind grey swirls of cloud and gives them a blazing line of silver. In patches where the sky is clear, the stars shine bright as jewels and the faint breeze accentuates their twinkling. A shower comes down in large drops and makes wet circles on the road, and soon is ended. There are flutes among the trees that make a beautiful sound against that of the river; they move among the trees and go beyond the curve of a hillside, fading impeccably away. Villagers return home and some are singing as they go along, also entranced by the night. On the dark face of another hill is the palest form of a waterfall, lit by the heavens. Overhead clouds pass, leaving behind a Prussian blue sky, lighter than the mountains and hung with a white moon that gazes eternally among the stars.

Village boys play in the wheat fields, running from higher terraces in turns and falling on a soft manure heap below. Each tries to outdo the other, amid shouts, cries and whistles. Their game is soon done, and they walk past the fields chattering, up the hillside and into the forest to their huts. Two women carry planks of wood up to their homes, helped by a smiling three year-old. In the village, a small boy cries loudly. His exasperated mother continues up the hill and shouts after him to no avail, for he continues to bawl furiously, his face distorted in hysteria and his long hair straggly and damp with tears. He has the look of a midget in the forest and succeeds in irritating everyone with his hoarse crying. A passing woodcutter shouts at the boy to stop screaming and it only makes matters worse, for the child sits down on the mud with renewed stubbornness and yells louder than ever. A muddy, lonely dog saunters by unconcerned and goes further into the woods. A little distance away, among brick houses and apple orchards, a villager has set up a teashop, and it is filled with silent people drinking and smoking. In the sunlight, young boys have gathered into a circle to gamble at cards, and they argue and clap merrily when someone wins a round. They are a dozen years older than the boys in the wheat fields, but their banter and gesticulations belong to a universal age group that defies definition or a time frame. Women wash under a tap on the hillside, and from there, the path narrows and curves among the cedars, skirting the pond that can be seen not too far away. One comes to a clearing of mud, full of half naked children excitedly at play while some among them merely watch. Three or four women emerge from a tiny path, their backs laden with grass and twigs from higher slopes. An infant walks down the path all by himself, soon followed by a herd of black cows that stop to graze on grass, and are shooed by the old man behind them. The tapering path takes a bend and leaves a village among terraced fields below. Four children sit under a tree, clumped together, making a garland for an infant who is already decorated with a wreath of daisies and who smiles shyly. Young woodcutters have felled a tree that lies horizontally across a ledge of the hill; two boys hack at the trunk methodically, skinning the bark off to reveal yellow timber. Their axes glint new in the sun and their limbs shine with the sweat of their labour. A few boys look on, and below, villagers gather the twigs that have been severed away and make bundles of them for their hearth. A pathway is irregular with slabs of stone and skirts a wire fence under almond trees, leading to a small meadow with a view to opposite mountains. There is a small mud cottage higher on the path, and ahead, a few fields give way to apple trees and cedars that obscure the edge of the hillside beyond which spreads a marvelous view of slopes rising swiftly to trees above shale. This gives way to the fine band of snowy peaks that still have the sunlight upon them and shine far brighter than the forests below that are engulfed in shadow. Waterfalls seem closer at this height and they cascade more turbulently, yet still remain strangely silent. An old tree has grown enormous in the fields and the path veers around its trunk, dipping over a small bridge that has been laid with steppingstones on wet ground. Not far away, two curving fields have been sown with rice and glow brilliantly in the shadowy light among the ochres of other terraces. A crow glides low upon them and is gone beyond the trees. A helicopter flutters loudly through the hollow of the valley and disappears into a range of mountains, leaving behind a hush of breeze and the twitter of birds in field and wood.

Scree glitters, catching the sunlight exactly, and a nearby village is isolated on the giant mountainside. Flat shingle roofs reflect sunlight in a rare resonance with the stones that surround them. A waterfall is in shade, but treetops light up in the mass of blue-grey. The bus moves through villages and orchards and follows folds of mountains. Below the road, slopes are cluttered with terraced fields as if a patchwork quilt has been thrown, reaching out for kilometers ahead. Tiny village clusters are identical and placed randomly; there are giant boulders, sharp and flat-faced, peering through the bright spray of apple trees.

The temple rises not too high and is of grey granite, its top sloping upward in a shikhara. The sculpture of a black bull rests before it and its forehead is decorated with a single rose petal that shines on deeply weathered stone. Carvings on the façade are not too ornate, but rather belong to the village art of the region, yet have a fineness of feeling in the way images and creepers are rendered. On the porch way is another Nandi, no higher than one's knees, and a child sits astride it, playing on its ample back. Niches on the side have small windows filled with deities, each having a petal pasted upon them. A barred door guards the god in the sanctum within. Circling the monument, one chances upon a seated sadhu and his companion in saffron tatters who sleeps on the floor. A red triangular flag flaps on the shikhara, towering above the roofs of the village. Beyond, the mountains spread above a generously rolling valley. Past the courtyard is a tiny shrine made of the same granite, the intricacy of its dark carvings ravaged and obscured by the elements and by lichen that has clung to them like a white rash. A sapling too has rooted itself on the stone floor and flourished. One passes wooden homes on both sides of the path upward. There is another, larger temple in a clearing. The roof has been protected by a wooden pagoda-like construction and shelters it from rain and snow. The courtyards are empty and the doors locked. Further into the village there is a naïve cement archway with a saffron flag upon it, beyond which is another deserted courtyard. Looking back at the view of the blue hills, the asymmetry of the arch takes on a gracefulness as it frames two huts. Open sheds on a side of the courtyard of dry mud have a log of charred wood, and the image behind the temple door is bright with tinsel, even in the darkness of the interior. The outer niches contain images or sometimes just another stone slab swathed in saffron cloth. A sprightly brook runs downhill beyond the stiles that border the temple. The abandoned shrine exudes poignant charm and a vulnerability that welcomes the visitor for a moment of contemplation, or for the offering of a few flowers to the god within. The carvings do not bewilder or inspire awe, but rather compel simplicity of gesture even though it may be soon forgotten. In that lies the temple's mystery that perhaps came with the first foundation stones laid so long ago by local artisans. It does not possess the ever- growing mystery of the mountains, but contains one that is dormant and modest in essence, and for being such, is touchingly accessible to even the humble villager to whom it is addressed.

In other villages, girls sit in circles, playing in front of an old temple. The woodwork of the exterior has weathered and darkened to resemble stone, and beneath its roof sits a tired sadhu who looks vacantly out to nothing, past the games of children, past the rush and chatter of people in the small bazaar, past even the vast mountains. Perhaps he traveled through those very mountains from far away, and came to rest by his god for a few days before moving on. A mud field adjoining the temple is dusty with the stamping feet of boys playing ball. Their faces distort with shouts and the strain of the vigorous thumping of the ball back and forth, and they provide a contrast to the restful people at the temple. A small stone shrine behind the main temple is similarly incongruous and lost in the middle of the dusty bazaar.

The countryside upon the road is predictable in its elements. The sun bursts through gathering clouds directly above the ridge of the facing mountain and is not too high in the sky. It spills a wide band of pale amber dust upon a hill, lighting it uniquely against the grey haze of the remaining mountainside, binding a spell upon it momentarily. Wheat fields spread on both sides and the hills are ahead, rising grey and triangular out of the gold and green against a cloudy sky through which azure breaks through patchily. The late afternoon sun touches the hills obliquely so that two in the foreground are highlighted and the rest remain silhouetted. One hill is flecked with only a sprinkling of snow at its summit, and that too catches the sunlight and glitters blinding and magical white in the evening light. The twin hill next to it is abundant with snow, but because it has not captured the sun, fades mysteriously into a haze. Vast ranges of snowy peaks again come into view, their tops covered in a white cloud, as if an enormous curtain has been drawn from one crest to the next, framing the black-and-white stretch of inaccessible ranges and safely sealing in their ageless secrets.

A path of mud and stone mounts the hillside, continuing past small farms. For some of the way, one can see the river below, sparkle over rocks, and one is soon into the pines, chestnut and sycamore trees. The broad path thins, clinging to the rocky and muddy hillside as it goes higher. The view of the valley disappears, and all one can now see facing one is a sharply rising mountain. It is veiled in cedar and has green meadows perched at impossible angles that become shreds under the summit. Snow covered ranges blaze in the afternoon sunlight to make one's eyes smart with the glare. A breeze cools, and one comes to a small waterfall flying down rocks and thick ferns, making small pools above the path. Now the way becomes dangerous and ascends in vertiginous zigzags. Cobweb threads ripple from branches and shine in all colours of the spectrum as sunlight hits them. The way has been unused for very long, and the cobwebs have collected, unbroken except by wind or the falling leaf. The path straightens out, but is still narrow. One goes past woodcutters hacking at a felled tree, and there are shepherds. The goats that had seemed so awkward in the town now have grace and agility on the steep mountainsides, even where there is no grass. A stream flows through a slender and threatening cleft and the path swings giddily in its steep climb and disappears among mounds of mud and rubble so that one has to move cautiously. Each step is hazardous upon the soft ground that is strewn with chips of branches and slippery leaves. The slope becomes even steeper and the mountain seems torn to ribbons. Trees are dry and dead and stumps are charred. The ground of dark mud is littered with twigs and difficult to negotiate. The mountainside falls perilously and conceals all paths. The breeze itself seems to smell of danger, and one inches upward, blind to everything except the serpentine string of a path that loses itself under twigs and needles, able to be seen only by the most persistent and scrutinizing eyes. Broken rocks perch miraculously over perpendicular ledges, and at last, the ground becomes more spread out, so that one passes over to broader spaces with ease, again cognizant of the wilderness. There is a scooped out valley upon a high ridge, underneath a tree-covered mountain on one side and a snowy range on the other. Snow has fallen in rags over trees and cliff faces, and slim waterfalls in the rock body seem static in their gush. Water flows through the valley, but nature here has been cruel and ruthless; trees lie all along the grassy meadow like innumerable corpses, their large trunks overturned and their roots naked, having pulled up large rocks in their fall. Bark has fallen away in large scallops and the wood has become grey and dry in the open. Branches clutter the wet ground and are scarred with moss and fungus. Beyond the cedars that still stand is a view of snow ranges, but at one's feet lies a brutally battered stretch of land that breathes destruction amid the wasted skeletons of trees. In the late afternoon, buffaloes, sheep and horses moved to ridges that still had sun, but now they have all gone away. The sun lowers in the sky and the trees acquire an evening haze. Colours of the meadow melt with the darkness of foliage. Tops of mountains are covered in mist and the blue sky amasses with white clouds. Water that trickled over ground becomes a stream not too far along and makes its way over rocks, unmindful of the steep fall of hillside. In the fading light, the sounds of water become clearer and gnarled logs assume a sinister immobility. The sky becomes overcast and the mountains stand stubbornly. They are brooding and unconcerned with protecting one, and have almost been vanquished by the clouds that overpower the sky above. Mist gathers on their crest like a knot of thieves and hangs there, aged and menacing. There is a chilling wind on the ground, and in its strangeness, is unable to stir the leaves on the chestnut and pine. Darkness falls stealthily, the hills darkening to utter blackness against the lifeless light of the cloud-filled heavens. With it comes the magnified roar of the stream and a cold that seems to move even slower but with unearthly certainty, becoming more intense and all enveloping as night deepens. A fire burns quick and orange, exuberant and free of surrounding dross, the wood cracks to grey ash amid flames and embers in an easy transformation, oblivious of the fearful cold and dark that has overtaken each leaf. A moon wanes somewhere behind the thick canopy of clouds and is very late in emerging; long after the flames have turned to embers, it comes for a few moments, to be swallowed again by clouds, as if wary of the night. There are a few drops of rain, but those cease too, as if quelled by the cold. There is only an unthinking silence beneath the sound of the water, and a bitter, unfeeling danger that is in league with the staggering steeps that lured one here. One understands in one frail moment, how the ancient rishi had been able to cohabit with the wild beast in a wakeful silence in the bowels of a cave, both seeking protection from the elements. One understands perhaps the sacredness and force of fire in the unshakeable fury of the cold night, one understands the longing and love for the dawn, the precious and unfailing glow of the sky before the final radiance of the sun. In the dark, the moon has moved to the far edge of the hilltop, and shines again for an instant through a break in the clouds. It is soon gone, and a formless mountainside is again in the throttle of the dark. There is no thunder and no wind, only the burden of a heavy sky through which a lonely star glints and drowns, leaving behind the gnawing and numbing ferocity of the cold. The sky grows light in a slow, sure magic, snuffing the dread of night and the callousness of cold with its benediction.

Two small urchins appear as if from nowhere with a pail of milk, and stand silently by until the pail is emptied and returned with a coin. Then, tripping over dead branches and the water, they stop to pick yellow mountain flowers. They are soon gone to their tattered hut among the trees, leaving among their footsteps a conquest of innocence over the night on the mountain, and the vestige of an unknowable and renewing frailty.

The cedars catch the strong wind under the overcast sky; stillness also seem to come to them sooner than to other parts of the valley. The pond has shrunk and become old and has lost its pristine fullness. Its edges are not well defined any longer, but have a rim of slush that is uneven with dirt and footprints. The dark water is thick with needles and through clear patches, insects still whirr and make the surface shimmer, but it has changed, for the pond no longer has the will to respond to the twinkle of stars with delicate ripples at night. The rock no longer touches the receding water but stands aloof a little sadly upon the meadow, dappled in lichen, sprinkled with needles, and caked with pin cushions of old moss. A bird sings through the trees with a lovely song and that is soon overtaken by the hush of the wings of a large crow swooping down to branch stubs, cawing. People that pass through the forest are not lit by any sun; woodcutters appear, three boys chase each other laughing, a cowherd leads a score of black cows on the grass and a woman scrabbles the ground for needles and piles them into a basket. Iris has bloomed overnight, heads erect on tall stalks, fragile as they curl in and out of their centers. Tiny yellow insects swarm over pale violet petals and are indiscernible a foot away from the flowers. A sudden rent in the clouds lights the cracked bark of a tree, but the weak sun is instantly gone, like a signal or a remembrance. A white blaze high in the sky is the only hint that the sun exists, however frail and ancient through the thick layer of clouds. Ants and bugs crawl out of cracks and holes in the skull of a cow. The fields have been tilled and the brown earth has been turned up in drying clods. The countryside is in the midst of changing its robes, its moods altering to usher in a new season. And yet, one hour passes into the next with a naturalness that hides all change and the whistles of passing children and flutes in the night only put a stamp on the continuity of things.

A mud road leads to a valley high in the mountains. There are ranges all around as the valley narrows upwards, the tree line giving way to vertical cliffs above. It is rocky and there are sparse meadows through which a green-blue river and streams run. There are many waterfalls; some fall threadbare from fine clefts, cascading into a haze, darkening the rock around them and disappearing into the scree of the mountainside, while others are thicker and flow down gentler slopes. Shepherds lead their flock over wet hillsides that ascend to cliffs. Apart from them and passing cowherds, there seems to be no one and there is not even a village in the valley. A strong stream dashes over enormous rocks to meet the river between insurmountable cliffs. Further, there is a log across the water that leads to the path above. Two cowherds push their animals into the stream to get them upon the dead tree to cross over, and carry a young calf in hand. Goatherds follow, using the footbridge and go easily across, past the rocks that litter the way. An old unused road of stones and rock slabs winds upwards too, past the river and unmelted snow, disappearing somewhere over steep slopes to mountains beyond. Smoke still rises from ashes on the roadside, something that earlier shepherds have bequeathed the path. Ponies graze and above them are the white flecks of herds of passing sheep. Beneath the snowy peaks, a large waterfall cascades in white tatters. Over the meadow, a fierce river crashes down a sharp incline of rocks, its foamy body exhaling swirls of mist as it hurtles to take a swift turn to lower ground. Upon a hillock rest the vestiges of two huts that have been broken by the fury of the elements and stand strange in the deserted valley. They are merely two or three stonewalls with holes for windows, but no roof or floor. Nearby, the sun and snows of winter have upturned gnarled trees. They are dry as bone and unmoved by their environment and immovable. To a side, a semi-cave has been hewn out of an enormous rock, its inclined roof blackened by the fires of cowherds. Upon ground below it, flat rocks form an uneven floor and refuse thrown upon it betrays its use by nomads as a resting place on cold nights. The clouds cover the snows and change the light in the valley, so that certain parts reflect sun while cliffs remain in shadow. The afternoon moves in patterns of light as if under a spell. A small caravan of donkeys passes with a family of nomads leading them. They halt above the meadow and undo the ropes of their utensils and sacks of grain on the backs of their animals, to make a meal. Some villagers come over the high pass, past the river, over the stream, and soon are gone. Bright birds fly from rock to rock over the river, their song unheard over the sound of the water.

The cedars are utter silence in the dusk and the sky behind them turns glowing beige. Silence spreads in the forest and seems to reject all noises, pushing away the voices and whistles of children and the sounds of the town below. The dying pond has become even smaller; weeds that grew on its bottom now peer above the water, blotting out the shine of the surface with their green. Only in one part does the water reflect the trunks of cedar or the glow in the sky. It seems as if the pond has been snuffed out by the season, and wants to leave in quiet. The shield of trees around it stand as if in attention to its passing away. Villagers no longer wash in it and impish children no longer play by its side. Dragonflies have deserted it and even the great rock has withdrawn morosely from it. Only the trees are left, standing in total stillness and they have covered it in needles to make for it a shroud. The skull that glows enigmatically in the low light seems to speak of renewing death and is static upon the grass. It is the brief season of the iris that blooms momentarily; the cedars know no season, for as one looks up to their sepia filigree against the sky, they seem to have wrested the strength of giving from nature and endowed the pond that glittered in their midst with their bounty. There will be more seasons, and the magic of a new pond that will collect from spent rain, and this will happen overnight. But for the moment, it is a time of farewell, and the cracked bark of cedars seems to hold that memory. Night falls, and with it comes sadness at the passing away of beautiful things. The path downwards is lonely and its stones are bordered with a faint futility.

A Verdant Valley

A Verdant Valley

The brilliant sun is more heat than light and blazes the dust. The train is in the last platform, past corridors, ramps and crowded bridges. Names pasted on the list on the train door are usually misspelled, but nevertheless indicate a reserved seat. The compartment vibrates with fans and porters carry trunks and bedding rolls on to benches. On the platform, a sadhu has spread out his cloth, conch, Ramayana, bell, brass image, pot of water and sacred thread, and is praying. Someone has lit his oil stove and made his family a gruel lunch. Others wash their clothes under a tap and have a bath. Policemen play cards. Army men stand around drinking tea in their underclothes, and the tea man refuses to serve any more tea, as he is moving down the platform to meet the rush at the next train's arrival. People have made the station their camping ground. Children lie around in torn clothes. Fat old men scratch, and an army man changes from his nightclothes into his uniform in the middle of the day. A bearded priest bathes in a loincloth and as he swings his cloth around to change his clothes, the wind lifts his lungi. A man chews a mango that hangs out of his mouth and throws the skin and seed on the floor, missing a passerby's foot by an inch. Women bunch up their saris as they scrub and scrape cooking utensils, and men hoist up their pyjamas as they cross the tracks. A young officer searches for someone to chat to. Surprisingly, there are no cows on the platform. The last carriage of a train draws up to a wooden barrier and bumps to a halt. A boy rubs the wheels of his toy airplane and lets it rattle across the floor where another child picks it up and sends it back with a grin. Army men toss sleeping bags that are of the same green as their clothes, setting them against the tracks, and then walk off with them on their shoulders. Some carry water pitchers of clay as well. Sparrows flutter past wires in uneven numbers. A group of people argues vociferously and without halting in their step. Young men with shiny plastic rings seem curious as they fidget with their fingers. Someone gargles and spits out water. Porters push empty metal trolleys that jangle on the ground. A seasoned old beggar hobbles by, balancing a thimbleful of turmeric on his palm. A man combs out his hair and at each turn shakes out the water from the teeth of the comb. A fat man spins a handkerchief to shoo flies. An old hag moans mournfully as she turns over in sleep. Graceful women wearing no blouses underneath their saris carry pots on their heads, as if returning from the village well. A dog carries a piece of fur in its mouth, followed by another dog with a pink and dripping tongue hanging out. A smiling paan maker talks about the time he accepted a counterfeit hundred-rupee note. The train fills up. Passengers take their seats, talking and wiping the sweat from their faces with wrinkled handkerchiefs. The train budges wheezily, and children shout excitedly. A bright boy peers out of the window looking for the clock on the platform under the shed, and proclaims that it is not yet time for the train to start. Elders sit facing each other, talking about thieves on trains. One of them recounts how he had handed five rupees to a tea vendor at a station and how the train had moved on, leaving him with a five-rupee cup of tea fuming in his hands. What was worse was that the same thing had happened to him at the next station, except that he had run out of fivers and had paid ten for the second cup. There is laughter, and then the conversation focuses on the little girl whose ice cream has drooled on to the seat, with her looking vulnerable and ready to break into tears through heavy mascara. But she decides to squeal instead and insists on sleeping on the floor at night. The fans go off and the air becomes still and the heat insufferable. The father assures the children that the engine is being attached to the bogeys, and sure enough, the fans whir on again to everyone's relief and to freshly wiped brows. A policeman in khaki looks into the compartment with no interest whatsoever, and there is the clatter of trunks being slid under seats nearby as boxes collide on heavy metal doors. Outside, the light draws harsh shadows on walkers, and further down, an overhead shed throws everything into a cooling shade. The saris on women and the white shirts on men become blue and grey in that shade, and as they suddenly emerge into sunshine, they appear to have been set afire. Vendors walk into the train with shrill and guttural cries. A magazine seller balances forty books in his arms. One of the men in the compartment says it is time for the train to move and exits, reminding the group to drop a postcard home as soon as they reach. He has read the names on the door and asks someone to look after his family on the journey. Soon he is outside, patting his ice cream daughter on the head through the iron grill, and he turns his head aside to spit on the burning platform of stone. On a further platform, piles of gunnysacks make ochre barricades, and are stuffed with cotton that spills out of rips in the sacks. Light changes with evening pressing on, and a flock of pigeons floats in curves repeatedly over sheds. The light in the sky charms each form upon which it falls and has relinquished the harshness it had in the day. Despite the din of trains and the noise of people, the evening seems to bring quietness. The train soon pulls out, and the station noises fade as steel wheels lurch on to a hot and open countryside, past industrial suburbs. The children have exhausted themselves with shouts and screams, but their excitement and curiosity wears its effects on the mothers. Lights come on as the sky darkens, and the journey assumes a force of its own in moving forward.

The long road winds like an endless grey serpent, and in a few hours, there are mountains. The range spreads all round, and its immobility against an even and bright sky strikes one as having a strong presence. In the afternoon, upon turning a corner, there is mist that filters through a thick green forest, glowing strangely as it shields the grove from the sun. There is always a peculiar fragrance along with mist, a humid coolness that smothers every other sensation, and even on a moving bus, it is evident. In the clear again, one looks back to see the mist tumble downhill, floating over the trees and sliding down as it is sped by the breeze above. Crossing hillsides that are almost bare one sees rock faces that are stern and streaked, sculpted to a cruel clarity in the falling light of early evening. Mountains rise for hundreds of meters above the narrow valley and the road is far above a river that appears absolutely still, its ripples invisible and its swiftness obscured. It shines in places where the light catches the water, for it is mostly in shade, and loses itself among rocks to emerge further, toffee-brown and flat, as if the mountain had cracked open only to permit it a passage. As the bus continues, it enters the valley in darkness. It has been cold, but as one descends, it becomes warmer, and one can open the window again for fresh air. When one reaches the city at midnight, it lies folded like a mystery, only to reveal itself the next day.

Along the wooden steppingstones upon the lakefront, there are two giant Chinar trees, growing close together with only a tiny clearing of cool mud between their trunks. Boys walk past singing, and as one looks up to the branches, one cannot tell which branches belong to which tree. There is only a cluster of green; two seeds fell on the ground in the same way, hundreds of years ago, and their togetherness has expressed itself so long afterwards in the jumble of branches upward. Reflections of the rippling lake strike the leaves and they glitter with the translucent sky between foliage. The seeds fell by the edge of water, and the trees grew while the lake remained static. Lotus leaves shiver on the water, buoyed to the surface by webs and masses of weeds at the bottom of the lake, and tiny fish dart about among them. A boy shouts across the lake and his voice seems to land on the shore without a single ruffle.

The city unfurls before one without the colours and lights it had assumed in the late afternoon. There is a morning haze that shrouds it in sleep, yet already, there are many sounds. Over one area, a cloud trails low and obliterates rooftops and the enormous trees that tower above buildings and minarets of mosques, dwarfing all in grey-green. The lake glistens even in the early light, and the river is like two strings of silver ducking in and out of Poplars that go far into the valley. Nearby, roofs of houses seem piled on each other, dovetailed and sullen and exuding fine pipes of smoke that evaporate into the haze. An area of trees shields a red-roofed building and the sun rising over the hill falls in a pool against it yellow windows, lighting it uniquely as it rests against a softly greying landscape. There are hums and instant spurts of noise; the shrieks of crows overshadow the fragile cooing and twitter of mountain birds.

It had once been a magnificent temple to Vishnu and now it is a ruin. All that remain are large granite slabs and bases of pillars. Grass has grown along the courtyard and into the temple area; time has recreated the monument. There are vestiges of ornate carvings and here and there, wonderful figures pose in splendid doorways. Some pillars are carved in intricate patterns of leaves and flowers. There is great beauty and the perfection of proportion and there is also the strange feeling of a joy that has passed away forever. The years have shorn the temple of any roughness, leaving only an essence of refinement. They have erased the thoughts of men, the emptiness of kingly wealth, the pettiness of courtiers and the futility of ceremony, and retained only truth. Around the courtyard that is fenced in with barbed wire is the thoroughfare where the noise of buses is deafening. Ever-present vendors sell peanuts and raisins among the dust, and it seems for an instant as if the temple is bound within a spell of silence that the road cannot penetrate. Within its precinct that is but a few meters away, an unearthly timelessness holds sway that makes the temple an alien on the side of a bus route that has no character whatsoever.

There is another old village by the roadside that is a sacred place whose ambiance almost flows over on to the road in the same way that the shops in the village cannot contain their goods. A stream has been channeled into crisscrossing paths that are very shallow and weave in rectangles to two square pools in the spacious courtyard, and the sunlight through the overhanging trees is gentle, dappling the grass and giving the water an irrepressible glitter. The stone steps at the end of the pool lead to a temple in an open pavilion under the spread of a Banyan tree that appears strange in an enclosure of Chinars. The limpid water sets off every pebble in the bed and each tuft of moss, and there are hundreds of fish swimming in shoals, swirling from canals into pools, their dark and muscular bodies swishing velvet as they take swift curves. Pilgrims throw gram to them and they gather like bolts of lightning to devour each morsel; there is an excited quick splash above water and the clash of many heads and bodies, but soon order is resumed to their meandering underwater once the food has been consumed. White turbaned pundits sit under the trees and each has a saffron mark on his forehead; many are old and wrinkled and some go over to the visitors. Their job is to place the lineage of pilgrims by consulting their books, and they have done this for generations, meticulously noting down each name. Some of them sit writing family trees into long and thick books that are bound in red cloth. The books are hundreds of years old and several feet long, and their silken paper has yellowed and frayed at the edges, so that they look like serpents that the pundits have unfurled on their laps. They pen the names in Sanskrit or in Hindi into appropriate columns, and they do this quietly after enquiring the sir names of people. The pilgrims look on with the curious emotion that thoughts about one's ancestors evoke; there is all the pride of one's lineage and descent in their gaze, because they have found records of the flowering of their families, the proof of their nobility and stock. They feel privileged in having continued this tradition by visiting the temple. The pundits only have a love of knowledge and a revering of tradition written on their faces, and their hospitality is sincere as they offer cups of kahwa tea; they have performed a unique and valuable service to their community and have done it for centuries. The pundits own calves, and the animals have an expression of serenity on them, coupled with the docility that comes naturally to the young. The care bestowed upon them speaks also of the kindness of the owners who hold the animals sacred. The villagers are oblivious of the sanctity of the pools or the special aura of the courtyard. A woman washes her clothes by the stream and the soap entering the water makes the fish scuttle to the far edge. At the other end, an old woman bathes happily, but unmindful of the peacefulness of the precinct. It is just a place that the inhabitants always took for granted, and that is perhaps part of the secret of its being valued through times of plenty and being able to survive in times of hardship.

The road ends at the small village, and then there is only a path over a meadow. At the top, two fields are enclosed in high wire fences; their gates creak in the wind and have rusty locks, and quiet overcomes one. The mud path disappears under pine forest to a welcome shade from the strong sunshine. Gnarled roots of trees lattice the ground as if the life of the trees extends beyond their trunks; the path is like an old man's hand that is brown and thickly veined. The sound of the river remains while one no longer has a sight of it below. The way is soft with dried pine needles, and the fragrance of sap makes one's nostrils smart. Between the trees one sees more pines clustering the steep slopes of adjacent mountains and the path uncoils, becoming narrower yet stubbornly moving on. The river glows as a patch between trees once more and upward, snows shine, resembling the water's whiteness. The path narrows perilously over almost perpendicular ravine but widens out once more and supports chunks of rock that have fallen upon it. In the sunlight again, one wants shade, and the largeness of the mountains all round make a deep impression while one is moving further into the range. Shepherds in a long meadow wave from a distance, and one is reassured of the presence of humanity within the abundance of nature. One passes an area where large trunks of trees are being burned, smoking aromatically in the sun. The snows lie only a hundred meters above yet the climb would be impossible. Small glaciers have drifted down into the valley near the rushing river and are brown and mottled with mud and broken tree stumps. The river emerges underneath as if freed and rushes to join the rest of the water flowing past. At a point where the path winds downward, a fallen pine arches to form a gate as if to a forbidden land. The verdant valley has white colts grazing in its meadows, and the villagers one encounters indicate the way onward. At last, one comes to a small wooden bridge that leads to a high meadow beneath shining snows. A couple of birds swirl high in the sky, and the mountains are wooded except in a part where a whole cliff seems to have fallen away, revealing strata of rock. Pines perch on steep faces of incline with a natural resilience, and the eyes seem wide open to the snows beyond, although the body is completely exhausted. In that exhilaration, one feels the strength that flows to the surroundings from the mountains, and finding tented accommodation, one nears to sleep as if cradled in unspoiled nature.

Darkness falls swiftly, within the span of an hour. The sun had fallen in a golden slant and bowed behind the mountains, bestowing its last rays to the snows. Everything else had been in shadow while a bird flew against the pines, white upon darkness. The wind makes no sound because it is gentle, and the turbulent river roars below. Isolated huts have lit their oil lamps and there are only two or three golden spots in the valley. Behind, in the field, a bonfire flies orange in the wind but there is silence everywhere. The half moon beams in a clear indigo sky, casting clean shadows upon rocks and giving the river a fluorescent sheen. The evening star hangs between two crags, a pendant carefully centered in the chasm of sky. The valley below rests in a fresh darkness and the forms of trees are black against the twist of river. Fields are stilled by oncoming night and the close mountains are awake in their vigil. The night air is new and untouched. The snows have the same brilliance in semi-moonlight as the river; these two are perfectly matched, the one an issue of the other. There are whistles in the valley that carry far into the night. In the dark, one discerns forms of running horses chased by shepherds to their stables. They whinny and stomp through lush undergrowth and are soon engulfed into the blanket of night and the stillness of the forest. The purity and power of mountains brings everything to rest, and even roosting birds become silent.

The last mountain blazes white in the morning light and is almost completely covered in snow, except for as area of brown rock that stands out like a cage of ribs. The way is stony and grassy until the snowfields. There, it seems as if all the snow slipped down the hillside to the level of the river, carrying in its wake numberless trees and rocks in devastating abundance. Then again, the snows covered up their brutality in a bland and uniform white. Upon the peak, they are still white and virginal, but the fallen glaciers are dirty with mud and glisten like mounds of grain in sunlight. Glaciers have cracked open to reveal white flesh. Water flows underneath, canopied by dripping sheets of ice. In one area, the destruction of the snows is unhidden; rocks are enormous, as if they had been rent from the mountain in a violent thunderstorm ages ago. There are hundreds of boulders, sprayed with vast quantities of severed pines that are ripped like so many matchsticks over stone and water. Above, the bald peak has new pines bursting upon it like a growth of stubble. The river rushes from gaping holes in the crevices of ice, spurning itself forcefully out of still ice. There is dynamism from stability, dead ice giving life to water as if suddenly rescued from a certain death. There is the serenity of glaciers releasing restless jets of water that are more foam than liquid. One is touched with fear at witnessing the spectacle of this laughter from stillness, the birth from unshakeable ice of stubborn, struggling streams bursting to their freedom from the immensity of peaceful frost, amidst the twisted and torn trees that have been dashed to splinters and strewn nonchalantly. There is the renewal of nature in the fullness of summer and thunder from sleeping fields. Where life begins, gentleness does not as yet exist. There is only elemental brutality and heedless urgency as a presence presses forward almost without feeling, consumed thoroughly in the overwhelming process of creation that can be seen all round.

Blazing Fields on the Bare Mountain

Blazing Fields on the Bare Mountain

T he upward mountain road becomes steeper, the river more blue and swift as it speeds over rocks. There is an open span of valley that is desolate and green except for a row of small shops along the road. Yellow flowers on slopes give the land a warm blush and up above, peaks display new snows. Further in the valley are bits of glacial snow like soapsuds that have not disintegrated. Trees are torn asunder on sharp inclines and lie strewn about, some having fallen into the river. The destructivity of an apparently gentle and verdant nature comes as a surprise. The narrow mountain road continues to skirt the river, leaving the wide valley to become lost under the snowy peaks. Forests of vertical pines grow on nearer ranges, but the road climbs yet higher uncoiling through rigid ice walls of glaciers that have been cut to make the way. Trucks with pictures of the Taj Mahal, flying tigers and snowy mountains hiding a setting sun ply slowly along the route, their exhausts alien to the pristine air. As the trail mounts, the river becomes tinier, until, from a hundred meters up, it appears no more than a blue and silver string in green meadows. Pines look like dark green needles that have been compelled by a magnetic force to stand vertically on a sixty-degree slope. They cluster like a closely-knit family, yet there are some that have dropped away from the clan and grow separately, as if scrutinizing their lineage up to the very summit of the mountain that is a mere crag. Impenetrable granite overwhelms the eyes and one cannot look for too long at the enormous fields of ice at the tops of mountains. Glaciers have been severed at the roadside and under meters of snow, the water trickles on gravel. Clouds rolling over the summits are white, but not as white as the snows; they are ethereal against the solidity of snow beds and their lightness belongs to a world that is apart from the stability of earthly terrain. The stratum of rock rising angularly appears vanquished in its ascent by the azure of the sky. The bus passes over perilous ridges of bald crags into the heart of peaks, and soon even the glacial beds are below one. Tunnels have been cleft in the ancient ice and its textures upon rock become graphic in the sunlight as if a wintry hand had spun and spread fine muslin, taut upon peaks as it stretches in some places and is sensuously folded in other parts. The glacier slopes upward in an arc and gathers into mottled lumps around an edge. Along the middle, ice has cracked open, showing a shadowy body and through its fissures, water flows to the ground opaquely blue and without a ripple. A river is in creation and is as yet motionless. Its birth is invisible, imperceptible and a secret of nature. The glacier that gives it a touch of life spreads for kilometers and there are vast fields where the snows of winter melt, showing rocky earth. Upon a plateau, countless streams dribble to lower ground and gather as they move onwards, becoming more vivacious. The melted ice is as yet to decide its gravitational course and is in the midst of becoming one current. A few hundred meters ahead, it will have found its energy and channeled it into a surging torrent that sweeps all in its wake.

The pass of the glaciers is left behind to reveal spacious valleys, green and gently inclined, laced with a network of streams. Shepherds tend to grazing sheep and a few horses and colts drink at the icy streams and at pools where the water has collected. The bus continues downward and the sun lights mountains that appear unapproachable once more. Those ahead are barren, huge bodies of rock that never could support any life. The wind in the afternoon is pleasant and dry and blows over low slopes that are dotted with clumps of grass, growing at set intervals on the vast surface, as if an unseen had had planned their planting. Going upward into a new range of hills, the water that has split to this side of the glaciers now widens and gathers into a turbulent ribbon of sandy grey liquid. One passes several villages that are cubicles of mud with tiny square windows piled upon the ascending slopes. They are bordered with clumps of trees, the willows slanting at their branches against sunlight so that they appear as if permanently windswept. Finally, winding through kilometers of bare country, the bus turns to show valleys tucked between high mountainsides. After the austerity of brown mountains, the green of wheat fields and trees burn with familiar earthly riches; terraces of crop are like so many handkerchiefs of thick velvet, ringed in by orchards of apricot and mulberry glistering in the breeze. Huts with square flat roofs seem to have arisen out of the soil itself, camouflaged upon rocks and sheltered by trees. In a field, a farmer tills his soil, with the yoke pulled by yak; the black beast and the farmer's dark clothes are carved against the ripple of green. The sylvan plenty of green comes abruptly to an end at the level of the mountainside, for above the line of trees, as if intuitive of an all-embracing absence of life, there looms only bare rock, strata etched cruelly as if the heart of a mountain had been split open. In the evening's changing light, the green glows even more vividly. It seems as if the mountains had conspired for one brief kilometer to accentuate the wealth of green upon their own relentless monochrome. Slanting sunlight scalpels each stone in the fields of gravel to chiaroscuro, as if possessed by its own charm. The last rays lend light only to a snow-sprayed peak, leaving everything else submerged in shadow. The powdery spray seems transfixed under a spell of the changing hour, and yet the sky remains curiously resilient in its colours to the setting sun, its bland and vast blue complementing the hot shades of rock. There is a premonition in those colours of the cold night that will soon overtake the warm plethora of stone.

The village one reaches is dark and its oil lamps flicker weakly on to the dusty street as the bus halts. Crowds have accumulated at the door of the bus, and men in white turbans offer rooms to travelers for the night. One filters through the jostling and shouting crowd to a nearby inn, ducking through tiny doorways. In the morning, the bus unceremoniously moves on again, passing over a wide basin that reflects the sunlit mountains above as water flows gently on its sand bed, overlooked by settlements protected in the harsh dunes of gravel by green fields. Countless ranges of fiercely wrinkled mountains can be seen along the route, the rock at times turning dramatically red or black. Sometimes an entire cliff is purple, and another surface near the road sparkles with minerals. Stilled avalanches of scree take on crème-coloured facades, and slopes smoothen under sand-fine debris. Between ravines another village shines, and one passes a rare bouquet of flowers on a bush that shocks the eyes with its pinks. The clothing and the features of local inhabitants change as one goes deeper into the mountains. The change in the people, as with the landscape, has been gradual. People's homes and clothes too have blended harmoniously into the environment. The snows and fluttering streams have relinquished their power over new terrain that is an immovable desert of rock. Peaks that seem as if talcum snow had been dusted upon them bequeath the land with rivulets that have trickled back to villages left behind; now there is scarcely a line of water to be seen in the parched countryside. Darkness brings a chill wind as the bus rolls through glabrous plateaus to the oasis town high above the world.

At dawn, ahead of the mountain birds, one takes one's first steps on to the street. One notices that there are no crows at this height. It is a solitary street with few alleys or parallel roads, and that is what the entire town consists of. Two roads trail off into the villages and into the mountains, but that is all; yet the town provides the hub for inhabitants for hundreds of kilometers around, and sees to their needs in every season. The light has just come into the sky, and it is too early even for the milkmen; the entire town lies before one to be discovered in the privacy of being there alone. Wooden buildings bordering th street are low two storey boxes, their fronts closed with shutters, padlocked and bound as if in awe of the cold night. The glow in the sky distills a shadowless light that still speaks of slumber. The air is fresh and fine and will be a presence one is always conscious of on this platěau so high in the mountains, and it seems to have vitality and the quality of being newly born that lasts throughout the day. The thick, small windows by the roadside hide behind the electric wires that hang over roofs of shops. In the distance, there are cubicle houses piled on the slopes until they end in a large earth-coloured palace that is crumbling, its wooden beams jutting out against the pale sky. Frayed prayer flags flutter mildly in the morning breeze at the transformed summit. Beggars on the pavement emerge from their patchy quilts like disheveled chrysalis and have instinctive grins as they shudder and rub themselves awake. They set about collecting twigs and leaves from the stony path for a small fire to make tea. The sun has come up over the hill, and with it appear the people of the early morning. The man who works at the post office breathes deep as he drums his fingers on the wooden ledge of his balcony and tosses yesterday's crumpled newspaper on the road. A few shopkeepers begin unlocking rusty doors, and display, even at this hour, the busyness of shopkeepers, although it is still a few hours before the market opens. Policemen clatter on the asphalt with metal buttons nailed to the soles of their boots, and soon the trucks thunder in, emptying sacks of wheat and baskets of vegetables brought from far away to fill the stomach of the town. Bedraggled children waddle onto the street from shaky by lanes and sit sleepily on the sidewalks against the trees. Creaking windows on first floors open to scruffy heads poking out for a whiff of morning air. The town awakes in half an hour as one sits on a ledge, and seems to have swung easily into full activity. Villagers swathed in long flannel robes tied with waistbands carry baskets on their backs, and there is the hum of conversation amidst the bus noises and metallic footsteps. Teashops have lit their fires and their kettles steam. Radios spin both music and speech, and there is the blip of a needle trying to place a popular station that can be left on all day. More peasants appear with packed donkeys, and the marketplace comes into its own, with too much happening for the eyes to absorb in an organized manner any longer. Small boys pull yaks by ropes slung through their nostrils. They are curious creatures, like black furry cows with sharp long horns and eyes like star sapphires. The sunlight is strangely sharp at this elevation and is crystal clear, lighting forms and adding a nimbus of gold to each thing, throwing neat shadows on the road against doors and lattices of old wood and bringing rough and mottled textures to stone and plaster. The people about the market move at a slow pace. There is an unhurriedness that comes with being very high above the heat and dust of the plains, and it gives the street an atmosphere of theatre. The clothes the people wear are unique but strike one as a little strange; top hat-like headdresses swerve above both ears like fin: and accentuate one's impression of being on stage. People look abou themselves silently and are not engaged in conversation with each other, and seem to belong to an internal world of their own. Many hum little tunes, and their smiles are always ready, as if they have just been waiting to burst up to the surface. The smiles pucker up high cheeks and turn eyes to slits instantly, and are all the more charming for being there for no reason at all. The spontaneity of their expression cannot help but communicate a friendly happiness, but their smiles do stop short of giving the feeling that there is something deeper in them: there is no tale to tell, nothing to relate in words, and there is no closeness. Yet there is profundity, and that is the effect of the involvement in a private and simple world that they always seem to have access to. Old people seem more numerous than the young, and are surely the more beautiful. Wrinkles on their faces are deep and profuse and give depth of character that the young lack, and their small eyes are invariably greying with age. The features are the result of years lived in the mountains in intensely dry air and brilliant sunshine. The teeth are always yellow and crooked if they are there at all and there is evidence of the long toil of years on their limbs and torsos. One enters a shop to buy a thing or two, and one has no change, but only a big rupee note. The shopkeeper says it will be paid for later, and does not expect the money immediately. In his small transaction, he points to the honesty and simplicity of the people who have no inkling of commerce and certainly no idea of market maneuvers. It would seem as if the environmental austerity had heightened a quality in the people that one normally finds only in children; there is an unknowingness of the ways of the world that has found its own protection in being able to survive within reality, and yet one fears that this may not last too long into the future of a society that is changing and becoming more aggressive in its modernity. The very lack of colour in the surroundings and the difficulty of obtaining materials make for a beauty that compels simplicity. The stones of the vast mountains are brown, and the facades of buildings are of the same rock and mud. The white of old plaster on walls is an occasional indulgence that speaks of the enormous effort of cartloads of lime having been brought from hundreds of kilometers away on mountain paths long ago. There is a blessedness that comes with the absence of garish paint that one has gotten used to elsewhere, yet one wonders how much longer it can last here. Wooden surfaces are often raw, and where they have been stained, it is a with a uniform dark brown, that is more out of a need to protect than to decorate. Facades are lumpy with stones and little lanes behind the road are wobbly and dusty. There is not the prosperity to indulge in smooth surfaces or in shiny glass, and over the centuries, graciousness in mud and stone has evolved into something of great character. There is never a drop of rainfall in the year, so the adobe of houses makes for the peacefulness of monochromes that meets the eyes everywhere. In contrast, clothes in shops are a blaze of colour, with shining turquoises and riotous yellows clashing with rich greens and burning pinks. When worn, they are covered by brown and black coats that dexterously hide the brightness of sleeves and collars, again only adding to the monochromes one is accustomed to seeing in the town. Very often, one comes upon old men sitting with prayer wheels turning in their hands as they look blankly on to the street. Women sit on the roadside with baskets of lettuce and turnips fresh from their gardens and their little toddlers bundled on their backs in

271

hammocks that sling across their shoulders. As the morning wears on, there are shoppers from surrounding villages and army men in uniform who go to teashops for a quick drink and then are back at work. Labourers weighed down with sacks finally set their burden down in front of shops and sink upon the pavement to rest their limbs. There is little or no sweat upon their brows in the strong sun because the dry air absorbs any moisture there is before it can settle into beads. The thin air is exhausting and one breathes heavily, naturally slowing one's pace as if the rhythm of the town has pressed itself upon one ever so subtly and persuasively. Schoolchildren come in bright uniforms and grins, cheeks chapped into brown dots and noses running, skipping on their way. At certain parts of the road, open pipes of gushing water have clusters of people filling jerry cans for their homes, and having the neighbourly chat as well. There are no taps, and the precious water trickles wastefully across the road. Old women hobble past, holding balls of cotton and distaffs, twirling coarse thread as they meander along shops. Yaks have replaced the cows of the plains, and two of them have come to loggerheads in a mock-fight, pitting their horns together in the middle of the road. No amount of horning from a lorry stops their playfulness, and within minutes a circle of spectators forms, egging them on. There are friendly smiles wherever one chooses to look for them, but little children unabashedly also offer empty palms for money. They ask for sweets or ball pens, but it is a game that is forgotten as soon as one walks past. Tourists do not seem to be looked upon as invaders into a private realm, and pose no threat partly because the inhabitants are unaware of the oldness of their ways that have been fixed through generations of habit. The slow pace that has settled over the town much like its rarified air brings about a naturalness and relaxedness in all transactions, and with it the shyness of people becomes a thing of rare charm. Garbage dumps are curiously without their signature stench and become almost entirely visual in character. One hopes that somehow the special air will also preserve the ways of the people, but the truth is that these mountains are becoming readily accessible to modernity with its uneasy gifts; as yet, in transition, there is a lucky equilibrium between welcome and nonchalance, between ancient simplicity and new comfort. Even the dogs seem docile, although often of the same breed as their ferocious cousins of valleys below. They sun themselves in the dust, only vaguely aware of passers-by. When the roads that connect the town to the world below are closed off due to snow or landslides, the marooned town becomes poor indeed, the supplies short, and the shops even emptier than they are now. That may be the perennial rhythm of the place, and this time of summer is a happy one that brings contentment. In tiny windows, potted plants sprout green leaves, and one considers how much one has taken flowers of the plains for granted; bright pink petals on a sill swerve in the breeze and evoke sadness.

A road from the town goes downward and leads through stark country. The sun is strong even early in the morning, and as the hours pass, it etches forms of rock and gravel with harsh clarity and throws distinct shadows. There seems to be no way to measure distance with the eyes, or the dimensions of the rocky plateau. The road is merely a line pressed by jeeps and trucks that have crossed earlier. In the middle of the plateau, the land slopes upward to mountains some kilometers away where the strata ascend dramatically. Before the eyes reach the craggy peaks that circle all round, one notices that bland earth colours have suddenly come alive in purples and greys, with bold gashes of dark rock embedded in the softer tones of other layers. Between the flatness of the rock-strewn plateau and the slopes is a rising foothill area, naked and barren too, but streaked with deep and narrow clefts where the snows of winter pass to become the brown and opaque rivulet that runs through the land. It is a windless place, and as one drives past, one leaves behind a cloud of dust that rises slowly into the air. Lowing over a mild slope, there appears a village in the distance, ringed in with Poplars and fields and sparkling with mud-coloured houses and terraces, with a palace on top of its highest hillock. Climbing up to the palace, one is careful of jutting crags on the rocky path. The stones of the walls are of the same colour as the gnarled rock faces upon which they stand, and they can be seen only because their builders endowed them with a smooth texture. Here and there, a corner or a bit of wall stands on curving and inclined rock and is disintegrating into a ruin. Through the entrance at the end of a turn, one reaches an open courtyard that is walled in with tiny wooden pillars that support balconies. A high pole in the center is swathed in prayer flag rags that float idly in the wind. Groups of visitors cluster at the door of inner rooms. A grumpy man in flannel robes takes money as one passes the door to look in, and his expression strikes one as being incongruous to the atmosphere of fine austerity that the building impresses upon one.

The barren road mounts through threatening mountains, and in some distance comes to a grove of Poplar with a stream gushing through pebbled undergrowth. It has fed a field of trees in the desert and bathes the road in its exuberance. Naked crags seem even barer against the spontaneity of fine green leaves that gleam in the textured shade. Walking through the grove, the pattern of sunlight falls upon one's skin as if chequered, and one's arms faintly burn in the magnified heat and cool in its intermittent shadows. One has learned to walk slowly in this high place like its languorous inhabitants. Behind the trees lies the place of pilgrimage, yet, having crossed the arid fields, one feels instinctively that the pilgrimage is in the journey itself, and that the temple is underneath the unknown stones. There was an overwhelming silence throughout, except for the noises of the vehicle, and all that is forgotten instantly in the laughter of the stream sounding in one's ears. A tiny village emerges between boulders below the grove. Dark-cloaked villagers go about their business, and a couple of young girls walk over the pebbles holding a goat by the string between their fingers. Beyond the narrow path are the stern walls of the ancient monastery, shaded by slender trees and sheltered by the silent sky. It seems abandoned in the middle of the day, and there are neither animals nor visitors, as if the height of the mountains and the blankness of the pale sky had succeeded in keeping all at bay. The lane leads to an opening on the hillside. There are crumbled ruins and a few low walls enclosed in a dusty courtyard. The path curves around a wall past bristling bushes and leads to a shaky staircase of stones. Here, the hillside is dotted with tiny cubicles that must be the homes of monks. They seem pushed into place between massive boulders wherever they could be balanced, giving the stark mountainside an altogether manmade geometry. The settlements seem very old and were built at random, as if a set of dominoes had been tossed carelessly on a slope and then forcibly bunched together, to give them their present design. Thorns mesh doorways and serve as natural barbed wire to dissuade the wandering goat or yak. In corners under the stones there is refuse that has as yet to be cleared away. Tiny doors and windows are of wood that has wrinkled and adopted the colour of the rocks. The latches are stopped with medieval locks that are rusty and rough. Tattered handkerchiefs hang limp and translucent upon strings extended from poles and are imprinted with seals of fierce gods with saucer eyes and multiple limbs. No faces peer out of windows, there are no sounds of people indoors and no movement of any sort, and for a moment, a feeling of desolation sweeps over one. A thorny bush perches behind a slanting rock and supports a single flower. A small breeze stirs as one takes the pebble path below the enormous rock, careful not to trip and fall upon the pile of white thorn twigs of the terrace below. A sense of prehistory comes over one as one reflects that the terrain hides myriad fossils that would be of easy excavation, wherein one could read the geological story of the region. The huge edifice of the monastery juts angularly over crooked walls, protruding windows and the balconies of monk cells, yet is aloof. The strip of green grows nearly parallel to those walls, and beyond, the eyes are lost in the ruins of rock and scree once more.

A large wooden door stopped by an iron latch leads through a corridor into the monastery, and swings apart quite easily to enter. The courtyard is ten meters past the dark corridor and in open sunshine. Sunlight seems not to be able to come indoors, and curiously, sound does not carry much distance either. Ascending the corridor, one catches glimpses of people in the courtyard. Monks dance to music while they clap and shout out to each other, yet the sounds of their movements do not carry even to the corridor, and noises are restricted to the courtyard. It is no wonder that the place seemed abandoned; there seems no way in which sound can be transmitted in the rarified atmosphere. It stops short, absorbed by the very air. Monks clap loudly, and the music is not gentle, but blares with the clash of cymbals, drums and giant horns. In any other setting, they would be raucous, but here, they seem to contain the correct decibel content. The air, by its very scarcity, contains both light and sound as if instantly condensing them within itself. Twenty-odd monks swirl and beat hands to music coming from a threesome seated under the porch. A few child monks watch as the elders move, leaning against lumpy walls. Maroon robes fly in the sun, and the cries are rough and guttural and appear awkward from the mouths of monks from whom one expects only docility. The overwhelming desert that spreads below could perhaps propel fierceness too in any human beings who live within it, and it is there in the dance of the monks. Dust does not seem to rise although feet sweep vigorously along the mud floor. The cymbals, horns, drums, shouts, stomps and claps combine to create a primitive beat that nears the domain of music but stops short of melody. One has caught the monks at their dance unawares, and they do not seem disturbed, but continue their wailing and swirling as if there were no stranger about.

The rectangle is bordered on one side by a low wooden viewing gallery that runs the length of the wall, supported by thin pillars. The seated Buddha in niches decorated with lotuses is repeated endlessly in bright murals. A long pole stands in the middle of the courtyard, dressed in rags and gently flapping in the breeze. There are prayer wheels hanging on wires in various recesses in the walls, and some are made simply of tin cans and contain scraps of prayers on scrolls. Arrows painted upon them indicate the direction in which they are to be turned, for if they are moved anti-clockwise, they invoke devils and not gods and undo the work of so many generations. Leaning against one of the tiny painted Buddhas, one's eyes come in line with the serene half-open eyes on the image. Soon the exertions of the monks are at an end, and within moments, the courtyard becomes empty. In the silence there remain only a few monks who tarry a little longer before they too disappear through one of the doorways at the end of the courtyard.

A young monk enters a room at the top of a staircase, and one follows him on tiptoe, slipping through the heavy wooden doors before they are bolted from within. The monk smiles a wordless greeting, and since most monks seem immersed in their own world, the recognition is unusual; there is no curiosity, but only a gentle welcome.

Again, the darkness that seems to turn day into instant night engulfs one. One has taken off one's sandals at the door, and the floor is sticky on one's feet. The sunlight had not been warm outdoors, and here the coolness of the room does not surprise one. But the first sensation is not of the lower temperature indoor, but of breathing very old air. It is not a musty smell, because the prayer room is used every day; but the doors are habitually shut immediately upon entering, and that is probably why the air smells as if it had been there from the time the first stones of the monastery were laid. Darkness conceals forms, but even before becoming accustomed to the gloom, a sense of sanctity overtakes one. It is a special enclosure that has been used for prayer for thousands of years, and no one can come away without feeling its atmosphere of serenity, reserve and sacredness. The dark seems to exist to heighten that impression alone. A few splinters of light fall through cracks in the wooden ceiling and set afire beams and poles and the cloth objects that are slung around them. Scrolls and robes hang as if they have not been touched for generations, and in the center of the floor are very large cisterns of yak butter with wicks planted into them. A few small flames burn unwaveringly, and the smell is rancid and strong, its pungency filtering into the air. The other contrast one encounters is that of a heavy and ornate interior in the expanse of open and airless country. The monks have unconsciously succeeded in creating an atmosphere that is denser than the outdoors. The monk leads one to a painted statue of the Buddha behind a wooden grill. The head is meters tall and its features are faintly visible in the glowing darkness and show an expression that is absolutely still. It occupies the entire back wall of the room, and the torso extends to a floor below. The gold of the body has tarnished and become the colour of the wood, but the half-shut eyes are newly painted like lidless thin leaves and radiate peace enigmatically and unerringly. The strong neck is strung with semi-precious stones and numerous dusty scarves that cascade to the room below. Yak butter lamps cannot bring the dull surface of the image to sheen, and upon first glance, one has only noticed the two eyes. Wooden benches circle the statue and are set low upon the floor of the prayer room. Along three walls are tiny square shelves, each stuffed with gilt boxes and the paraphernalia of ritual: incense burners, scrolls, books, cloth and small lamps. The monk sits down to meditation upon one of the benches and casts another smile upon one before becoming absorbed.

The silence of the old room, the hesitancy with which it reveals itself, the smoke from yak butter flames that cake the ceiling and give the wood a slowly-formed varnish, the darkened details of painted surfaces, gods and demons, and frail mortals alike besmeared with soot, enormous or even tiny prayer wheels that have been turned endlessly but appear immovable when not touched, fragile gusts of wind that can never enter the chapels but remain outdoors occasionally stirring prayer flags: all this makes one stand still for a while, and one wonders how many countless thoughts have occurred within these precincts. There have been fearsome contemplations on multi-headed gods and their ferocious consorts, agile demons and fierce chimera, the thunder of cosmic wars and intricate and impenetrable levels of worlds, making a mosaic universe that shakes and steadies in turns. One reflects on the complex mind that is all too human, and has nurtured all this over the centuries in this sanctuary of bleak mountains in utter isolation that compels illusion through sheer loneliness and insecurity. Here is an oasis of the mind's harvest in a perilous waste of environment. Through years of repetition and ritual, the smoky layers of obscurity cake what may once have been a rich and splendour filled world of the imagination. Imagination perhaps has a value only in the moment it is formed; inventions of the mind enrich only when they are fresh and living, for the rest is lifeless. One is careful not to think more thoughts in the room, and so one exits, leaving the tassel on the heavy copper knob dangling as one shuts the door. One had wished only to observe, and in the open once again, one breathes full and deep. One revels in the joyful sunshine, but knows that the room also contains records that are invaluable to humanity that would learn its own history and secrets. Brightness dazzles everything to whiteness and one rubs one's eyes, as if one has seen too much, too soon. In the courtyard, a child monk grins impishly, and one winces back, the sudden sunlight making one grimace automatically. A moment of light has seemed to purge the thousands of years of mind in its blinding glare, burning away the imagination to a dark and unreal cinder. And yet, this may be just the sensation each monk experiences every single day until it becomes implanted in the soul, and perhaps this is his enlightenment. The child monk is immune to all that somber ritual, unaffected by its tedium; the slant in his eyes changes as he smiles and he becomes expressionless and for just a moment has the head of the Buddha that one beheld within.

Leaving the brown blur of ground, the aircraft ascends in steep abruptness over bare mountains to a cloudless sky. Soon, the crags are left behind too, and there are endless snow-covered peaks as far as the eyes can see. There is exhilaration at being above them; there is nothing but clear sky and the snows become a haze in the far distance. Viewing the innumerable ranges, one understands the isolation and preciousness of the high desert one has left behind, and how small a pocket it is in the enormity of dazzling snows. Below one there are areas of ice that are golden with age, and fields as fresh as purity itself. There are vast sheets without any texture whatsoever, and other parts ridden with folds and cracks, and from these, peaks soar as if dragging the snows behind them almost to a point where they could touch the aircraft. That is never to be, for the snows remain untouchable and eternal. Frozen lakes are embedded like tiny emeralds in countless glaciers; sometimes one sees many of them grouped together in a single place. Their stillness and tranquility bypass the hum of the machine, and one knows that they are too deep in the mountains to ever be known by man; one is above the home of the snows that are protected by thousands of ranges all round and they have always remained impregnable. Yet one has caressed and conquered them with one's eyes, and one realizes that it is only for a fleeting instant, for they too recede forever behind one. High wooded mountains overtake one's vision and loom mysterious after the blinding openness of sheer white. Rivers begin through clefts between ranges like frail silver threads leading down to green hills. Sudden clouds are swept above the darkness of the hills and have not been able to surmount the snows; they remain strangely horizontal and static in the sky, like hordes of white invaders that have been stilled in their march upward. The aircraft takes a sharp curve and continues its descent into increasingly verdant valleys, to a familiar earth and into known emotions.